garden
folklore
that works

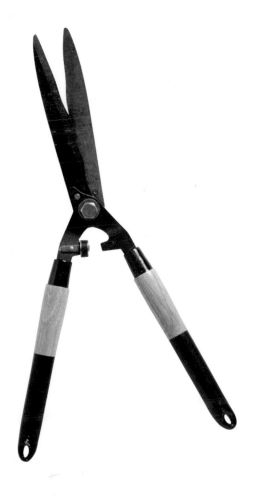

garden
folklore
that works

**Hundreds of practical, tried and tested
gardening tips collected through the ages**

Charlie Ryrie

THE READER'S DIGEST ASSOCIATION, INC.
Pleasantville, New York / Montreal

A READER'S DIGEST BOOK

Conceived, designed, and produced by
Quarto Publishing plc
The Old Brewery
6 Blundell Street
London N7 9BH

Senior Project Editor Nicolette Linton
Senior Art Editor Penny Cobb
Designer Sheila Volpe
Text Editors Peter Kirkham, Nadia Naqib
Picture Research Laurent Boubounelle
Photographer Paul Forrester
Illustrator Ann Savage
Indexer Dorothy Frame

Art Director Moira Clinch
Publisher Piers Spence

First published in 2001 by
The Reader's Digest Association, Inc.
Pleasantville, New York 10570-7000

Manufactured by Regent Publishing Services Ltd,
Hong Kong
Printed by Leefung-Asco Printers Ltd, China

READER'S DIGEST PROJECT STAFF
Senior Project Editor Delilah Smittle
Project Designer Jennifer R. Tokarski
Editorial Manager Christine R. Guido

Editorial Director Fred DuBose

READER'S DIGEST ILLUSTRATED REFERENCE BOOKS
Editor-in-Chief Christopher Cavanaugh
Art Director Joan Mazzeo
Director, Trade Publishing Christopher T. Reggio
Editorial Director, Trade Susan Randol
Senior Design Director, Trade Elizabeth L. Tunnicliffe

Library of Congress Cataloging in Publication Data
Ryrie, Charlie.
   Garden folklore that works: hundreds of practical,
tried-and-tested gardening tips collected through the
ages/author, Charlie Ryrie.
   p.cm.
   ISBN 0-7621-0299-3
   1. Gardening. 2. Gardening --Folklore. I. Title.

SB453 .R97 2001
635—dc21   00-045879

AUTHOR'S ACKNOWLEDGEMENTS
Thanks to all the gardeners who have helped and
inspired me over many years by passing on their
knowledge, verbal and written. Thanks especially
to my mother and to my gardening partner, Annette
Eaton, without whose practical advice and enthusiasm
I would probably still be stuck in the mud.

QUAR.GDF

CONTENTS

Introduction

This illustrated 15th-century Sienese version of Pliny the Elder's 1st century *Historia Naturalis* shows men cultivating an orchard and flowery meadow.

THE FOLKLORE OF PLANTS is in some ways different from the folklore of gardening. Gardens are relatively new; they were few and far between until the 15th century, but plants have always been crucial to life. Myths and folklore have surrounded plants at every stage, reflecting the changes in the relationship between plants and people, and in society, through history.

Garden and plant lore is so abundant that this book can only offer a taste, but it tries to show how some of the ancient beliefs about plants can be put to good use in your gardens today, and to illustrate that the old ways of tending your plot may often be just as relevant today as they were several hundred years back.

PASSING ON KNOWLEDGE

Even today, most gardeners probably learn much of their gardening knowledge from friends and relatives, perhaps later adding to the basic ideas by reading books and magazines and watching television programs. I know I picked up many of my gardening habits from my mother without ever questioning why such and such worked, or how. I just accepted something that was passed on to me. My grandmother might be astonished to find that I make tea specially to water the geraniums once a week, but she and my mother always watered them with tea leaves as a bit of astringent helped them to thrive in pots. The only difference is that I have more geraniums and less tea so the habit of using the leaves has turned into something more proactive. This is exactly what happens in folklore: an old habit or saying changes slightly through the ages until it is hard to see exactly where it came from. But there is still a reason for it.

PLANT LORE

Superstition and magic were an important part of culture in earlier centuries, and plants were crucial in all aspects of life. They not only fed, healed, cleansed, and often clothed, they also kept the home safe from evil spirits as well as diseases. Plants were indicators of changing weather and changing seasons in times before calendars and clocks; they punctuated all aspects of daily life. So all sorts of stories grew up around plants.

Many early stories invoked fear to prevent people from picking important or poisonous plants, or to keep robbers or strangers away; other stories were more positive. If we look closely at them, we can usually find at least a grain of truth – or at least a speck of reason. In the Middle Ages,

By the 16th century, most grand houses had formal gardens, although the range of plants was still quite narrow. This Flemish scene shows gardeners clearing, pruning, and cultivating in spring.

for example, there was a widespread understanding that the barnacle goose was the fruit of the barnacle tree. This might seem quite ridiculous to the modern mind, but it meant that the goose was plant, not meat, and could therefore be eaten in times of fast.

Plant knowledge has never relied on printed information, but on wisdom handed down for generations. Early housewives had to know a lot about wild plants before plants were tamed and brought into gardens, and it wasn't surprising that there was magic and superstition mixed with botanical knowledge. After all, it is remarkable that simple plants have the power to sustain life. It is extraordinary that they can cure your ills or kill you, turn you crazy or calm you down, quite apart from all their useful household functions in cleaning, fumigating, repelling pests, making cloth, oils, cosmetics, paper, and so on.

MAGIC POWERS

In an earlier era, where mystery and magic were part of life, the special powers of plants were once attributed to gods, or devils, or fairies.

LADY'S MANTLE

MIMOSA

Many of the old common names for plants reflect this: St.-John's-wort *(Hypericum perforatum)* is a beneficial healing herb; Devil's weed *(Datura stramonium)* can kill or alter a person's character; Lady's mantle *(Alchemilla vulgaris/mollis)* is a gentle healing plant named for the Virgin Mary; foxgloves or fairies' fingers *(Digitalis* spp.*)* were believed to be fairy plants, protecting households from evil.

Many theories and superstitions recurred through different cultures. The meaning of the saying "Flowers out of season, trouble without reason" seems an almost universal omen of bad fortune; while berried plants with serrated leaves like rowan *(Sorbus aucuparia)* or mimosa *(Mimosa* spp.*)* are always talismans of good luck, protecting from evil spirits those who grow them or wear sprigs of the plants.

FOXGLOVE

○ This illustration from a 14th century French illuminated manuscript depicts spirits of the Green Man entertaining nobles with dances, songs, and jesting to encourage a prosperous harvest.

PROTECTIVE SPIRITS

In pre-Christian Europe, festivals were important to give thanks to the spirits of plants. Images of a Green Man (a human head surrounded with a mass of leaves growing as hair and a beard) were popular, symbolizing fertility, inspiration, and regeneration. Jack-in-the-green was a garlanded green man figure created for pageants and festivals. In more recent folklore a less benevolent spirit appears, Jinny Green Teeth – an evil old crone who lives in water and grabs people who stand too close, pulling them under water and drowning them. She shows how myths have their uses, probably designed specially to frighten children away from the dangers of playing near water.

HEALING PLANTS

Most modern medicines are based on plants – the contraceptive pill is based on wild yam *(Dioscorea villosa)*; the opium poppy *(Papaver somniferum)* has produced painkillers such as codeine and morphine; the bark of willow trees *(Salix* spp.*)* led to the development of aspirin; and some antibiotics originally came from molds. Today, particular constituents are scientifically analyzed,

This 15th century illustration describes the belief that the mandrake would scream when it was uprooted by a mad dog, lured by fresh meat.

removed, and reformulated, but in past times most basic herbal remedies must have been discovered through trial and error. We have scientific processes to help us; in earlier times all sorts of theories were developed to try to predict the effects of plants. Many of these beliefs seem like extraordinary myths to the modern mind, but they arose according to the tools or methods of analysis that were common currency at the time.

Throughout the Middle Ages in Europe, people believed plants were effective for specific ailments according to variations on the principles of sympathetic magic – plants' healing properties were based on the way they performed in other situations. For example, yellow plants were said to cure yellow diseases, such as jaundice and liver problems; parasitic plants like mistletoe *(Viscum album)* were said to cure parasites on humans; the mandrake root *(Mandragora officinarum)* was said to aid fertility because it resembled the lower half of a man's body; and ivy berries *(Hedera helix)* were said to cure drunkenness because ivy strangled vines, and so on. It was also believed that wind-inducing foods like lentils *(Leguminosae* spp.*)* could be planted around the edge of a field to protect other crops from wind damage!

Native Americans had a well-developed understanding of the medicinal qualities of wild plants long before European settlers reached their country. Much of traditional Native American medicine centered on the activities of the medicine man or shaman, who took plants to induce a trance-like state that enabled him to communicate with the soul of the sick person and prescribe appropriate remedies. Remedies often came from plants today recognized as poisonous; their toxicity

Native American shamans underwent rituals to become one with the plants in order to discover an appropriate cure for a sick person.

meant they would have had a visible effect on the patient. Other remedies were not dissimilar from sympathetic magic – for example, many snake bite remedies came from plants where the root, leaf, or blossom resembled a snake's head. Many Native American practices gradually merged with those of the settlers.

In Europe in the 17th and 18th centuries, herbal knowledge was increasingly appropriated by special herbalists and physicians. They developed the "doctrine of signatures" to explain the healing principles of plants. This was sympathetic magic with divine overtones. It stated that all plants were stamped with some physical sign of their qualities. Plants with milky sap such as dandelions *(Taraxacum officinale)* were said to be good for nursing mothers or for male fertility; plants that grew in stone walls were said to be just as effective for breaking through kidney stones.

Lungwort *(Pulmonaria spp.)* was so named because it had spotted leaves that slightly resembled lungs, so it was used for respiratory problems. The flowers and leaves of eyebright *(Euphrasia spp.)* were seen as mottled and bloodshot-looking, so relating to the eyes. This wasn't really far removed from sympathetic magic, reformulated under a precise name to reflect the religious background of the time, with a beneficent God signing plants to indicate their powers. Although just-

SAUCE-ALONE

ified by appearances, the healing associations of plants were also based in part upon practice – so many remain true today.

Fifty years ago, few people were interested in herbal medicine. Now it's commonplace, and science backs up many of the traditional uses of specific plants. It's fascinating to look at some of the myths and mysteries surrounding plants, to discover the truths behind the myths, and when growing some of the plants in the garden, it's interesting to remember how long they have been used and appreciated.

NAMES AND ASSOCIATIONS

The old folk names of plants often offer valuable clues to the kinds of relationships people have had with them through the ages. Johnny jump-ups or wild pansies *(Viola tricolor)* were so named for their habit of jumping up everywhere, but in Europe they are called heart's-ease because they were used in a remedy to cure melancholy.

LUNGWORT

Soapwort *(Saponaria spp.)* makes an excellent soap, and is still used in some museums for cleaning delicate textiles. Pewterwort is an old name for horsetail *(Equisetum spp.)* because it was used as an abrasive cleaner for pots and pans. Teasel *(Dipsacus spp.)* was used to tease out woolen threads when weaving cloth. Numerous plants are known as woundwort or bugbane. Sauce-alone *(Alliaria petiolata)* was a staple wild vegetable for hundreds of years, with Good King Henry *(Chenopodium bonus-henricus)* deliberately so named to distinguish it from the poisonous Bad Henry, now known as annual mercury *(Mercurialis annua).*

PLANETS AND PLANTS

Astrology was part of people's daily lives through the Middle Ages until at least the 17th century, so it is not surprising that a good deal of plant lore is related to astrology. Plants were ascribed specific qualities according to signs of the zodiac. In deciding what planet ruled what plant, astrologers looked at the illnesses it treated, the plant's family, and the conditions in which it grew naturally. Plants that required a lot of moisture or grew in ponds were assigned to the moon. Plants that grew in dry places were assigned to Mars. Astrologers tended to ascribe plants to different planets, but the idea of planetary influences was common-place in 15th- and 16th-century Europe.

Many of the first settlers to America took this knowledge with them, where it was gradually transformed into a new form of garden lore. Planting by the signs of the zodiac is still popular in parts of rural America. Typical is the Pennsylvanian belief that cabbages sown in Aries, the ram's head, head up well, or that crops are large when planted in Gemini, the sign of the twins. Sowing in Virgo, the virgin holding flowers, is not recommended for vegetables but is for flowers.

Is this no more than sympathetic magic? Or stubborn adherence to folklore? Perhaps, but many of the ideas of moon gardening have been taken up by modern biodynamic gardeners who believe that plants are open to, and formed by, influences from the depths of the earth to the heights of the heavens. Biodynamic gardeners are returning to a much earlier tradition of

Garden activities in Aries or April, shown in a 15th century Bohemian painting, *The Cycle of Months.*

looking at the rhythms of the sun, moon, planets, and stars and the way these contribute to the life of plants. It is one aspect of a return to a more holistic way of looking at the world, where humans, plants, and the wider universe are all related.

TRADITIONAL PRACTICE

There were few gardens before the 15th century, but gardening techniques changed little for most people from that time until the middle of the 20th century. Then came the rise of chemicals and a change from traditional ways of looking after the garden. Before then, gardening knowledge was passed down from generation to generation, changing very little along the way.

Gardening used to be a subsistence activity, undertaken in order to feed the family. If your crops failed, the well-being of your family would be affected too. Traditional gardeners knew how to grow a productive garden, because they had to. Old garden lore revolves around the times to sow and plant, and the ways to keep your garden healthy – using what's around you. Now we can choose any plants we want, we can choose to grow food or not, we can buy composts and fertilizers, and we can construct a practical or a fantasy garden. But the principles stay the same.

More and more people are coming to realize that chemical-assisted gardening may not be all it's cracked up to be, so it's worth taking a look at some traditional ways of keeping your garden healthy. I have never used chemicals in my garden because I never thought to. It just never seemed to make sense. Some years, my garden is quite full of weeds by summer's end because they grow faster than I can remove them, but the soil seems rich enough to allow them their space without depriving the plants I've chosen to invite. There have been years when pests have feasted. But the balance improves year after year. I adapt some of the traditional methods to suit a busy lifestyle, and my garden and I rub along pretty well.

Gardening in the fresh air is a tonic, picking your own dewy flowers is a delight, and growing your own food is deeply satisfying as well as healthy and delicious. Growing plants with interesting histories or fascinating uses gives yet another dimension to a pleasurable activity. When you embrace the old and integrate it into your own way of doing things, you are continuing a pattern that has been unbroken since people first brought plants into their gardens. If your ways work, you will hand them on to future generations, contributing to a modern folklore.

CHAPTER 1

WHETHER THE WEATHER

"WHETHER THE WEATHER BE HOT, WHETHER THE WEATHER BE COLD, WE'LL WEATHER THE WEATHER, WHATEVER THE WEATHER." FORETELLING THE WEATHER HAS ALWAYS BEEN IMPORTANT TO PEOPLE WHOSE LIFE AND LIVELIHOOD DEPENDED UPON IT. PERHAPS THE FIRST WEATHER PROPHET WAS NOAH, WHO BUILT AN ARK BECAUSE HE CONFIDENTLY EXPECTED FORTY DAYS OF RAIN. EVER SINCE, PEOPLE HAVE BEEN TRYING TO CONVINCE OTHERS THAT THEY CAN PREDICT THE WEATHER.

MOST RELIABLE FORECASTING METHODS ARE BASED ON OBSERVATION BY FARMERS, HUNTERS, AND SAILORS, BUT PLENTY OF WEATHERLORE IS ALSO DEEPLY ROOTED IN SUPERSTITION, WEATHER RHYMES, PROVERBS, AND MEMORABLE SAYINGS.

SOME ACCURATE WEATHER PREDICTIONS BASED ON OBSERVATION OF THE SKY WERE COMMON SEVERAL THOUSAND YEARS AGO. MEMORIZE SOME OF THE OLD RHYMES AND YOU TOO CAN BE A WEATHER PROPHET.

Sky watching

"RED SKY AT NIGHT, SHEPHERDS DELIGHT. RED SKY IN THE MORNING, SHEPHERDS WARNING."

This is probably the most famous of all weather sayings, and is usually true. It has been repeated in different forms throughout history: "When it is evening ye say, it will be fair weather for the sky is red. And in the morning, it will be foul weather today for the sky is red and lowering" *Matthew 16:2*. 16th-century weather prophets preferred "A gaudy morning bodes a wet afternoon," and a later rhyme suggests "Evening red and morning gray will set the traveler on his way; but evening gray and morning red will bring down rain upon his head."

A red sky at sunset or early evening indicates clouds to the east, with clearing on the western horizon allowing the setting sun to be seen. Because bad weather typically comes from the west, at least in the northern hemisphere, a clear western sky can mean fair weather ahead. A morning red sky means the eastern sky is clear, but the rising sun's light is shining on clouds in the west, which are likely to advance eastward and bring rain with them.

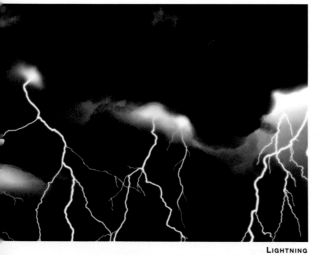

LIGHTNING

"BEWARE THE BOLTS FROM NORTH OR WEST. IN SOUTH OR EAST THE BOLTS BE BEST."

This is also reliable because weather generally moves from west to east. Lightning to the north or west usually means a thunderstorm coming toward you, but lightning in the south or east means it has passed by. "Rainbow in the eastern sky, the morrow will be dry. Rainbow in the west that gleams, rain falls in streams."

This is usually accurate for the same reasons. The time of day a rainbow appears is also an important sign. A rainbow in the morning (that is, in the west) usually indicates more rain to come, but a rainbow late in the day (in the east) suggests rain has moved on.

EARTH, A WATERY PLANET

MOONSHINE

The moon has always been eagerly watched by country folk, as an indicator to the weather and also of suitable times to plant: "When a halo rings the moon or sun, rain's approaching on the run" or "The moon with a circle brings rain in her beak." When a thin, whitish veil of cirrostratus clouds passes in front of the sun, or the moon, a large rainbow-like circle appears, with red on the inside and blue on the outer layer. This circle or halo is followed by wet weather about 65 percent of the time because cirrostratus clouds are usually followed by lower clouds and rain. This is most likely to be true during warm weather rather than in midwinter. It is also believed that the further away the halo, the sooner it will rain: "Circle near, water far; circle far, water near."

"Pale moon doth rain. Red moon doth blow, White moon doth neither rain nor snow." A pale moon is a watery moon, a red moon reflects the setting sun and can indicate a change in atmosphere, and a white moon shining brightly in a clear sky usually indicates settled fair weather.

SUNSET

The color of the moon can indicate settled or changing weather conditions. Colors are particularly accurate in a winter sky. A pale moon hints at rain, a red moon suggests a change in atmosphere, and a bright, white moon implies fair weather.

CLOUDS REFLECT EVERY CHANGE IN PRESSURE, TEMPERATURE, AND HUMIDITY. LEARN TO RECOGNIZE THE DIFFERENT CLOUD FORMATIONS AND USE THEM AS BULLETIN BOARDS.

Clouds

LOOK UP

"If fleecy white clouds cover the heavenly way, no rain should mar your plans that day." Woolly or fleecy white clouds refer to cumulus clouds. These are puffy but fairly dense clouds with dome-shaped upper surfaces, resembling balls of cotton. If they appear alone in the sky, this usually means fair weather.

CUMULUS CLOUDS

Cumulus clouds ◐

Cumulus clouds, however, often change into cumulo-nimbus. These are high and billowing clouds that swell and change shape to become increasingly heavy and vertical. They mean rain and often bring thunderstorms because they are most common on warm summer days. The Zuni Indians predicted "When the clouds rise in terraces of white, soon will the country of the corn priests be pierced with arrows of rain." Common weather lore suggests "Mountains in the morning, fountains in the evening," and "When clouds appear like rocks and towers, the earth's refreshed by frequent showers."

Cirrostratus clouds

Cirrostratus clouds cover the sky with a thin, whitish veil. If they turn into cirro-cumulus, fair weather is likely. Cirrocumulus clouds are streaks or patches of small white flakes like ripples or fish scales. They rarely appear alone but develop from cirrostratus or turn into other cirrus formations, hence "Mackerel sky soon wet or dry," indicating the likelihood of change. Or you may hear that "A dappled sky like a painted woman soon changes its face."

CIRROSTRATUS CLOUDS

Magnetic cirrus ◐

Much old weatherlore comes from sailors, to whom reliable weather forecasting meant life or death. "Mackerel sky and mares' tails make lofty ships carry low sails" is a centuries-old saying. The mares' tails refer to trails of ice crystals blown in streaks from cirrus clouds. These clouds usually appear ahead of an approaching storm or frontal system, and can indicate strong winds. In combination with cirrocumulus clouds, they foretell stormy, windy, wet weather. They are sometimes called "magnetic cirrus," as they are accompanied by magnetic disturbance in the atmosphere, and therefore turbulence.

Bull's eye

A small, increasing white cloud about the size of a hand is a sign of a storm approaching, as it means that pressure is building fast. In the Tropics a small, fast-growing black cloud, known as the "bull's eye," appears before hurricanes.

BULL'S EYE

CIRROCUMULUS CLOUDS

MACKEREL SKY

FORECASTING TIP

Cirrus clouds are delicate clouds with ragged edges that appear high in the sky. Look for rain or snow within 24 hours of cirrus clouds appearing and thickening, then giving way to lower clouds.

Watch out for bad weather, when quickly moving clouds increase and move lower, also when clouds move from the south and southerly wind picks up.

MYTH BUSTER

If you find the clouds difficult to read, listen to your body instead. "When your joints all start to ache, rainy weather is at stake." This is a very reliable personal indicator, often quoted as part of weatherlore. It is a sign of a rapid fall in atmospheric pressure, heralding stormy weather. Also scars may start to itch in this situation.

BIRDS, INSECTS, AND ANIMALS CHANGE THEIR BEHAVIOR ACCORDING TO THE WEATHER. THEY SEEM TO HAVE BUILT-IN FORECASTING ABILITIES THAT WE WOULD DO WELL TO HEED. BIRDS ARE PARTICULARLY RELIABLE ORACLES.

Birds

NORTH AMERICA

Nova Scotia

Mexico

Panama

SOUTH AMERICA

⊙ Swallows winter in South America, then fly to Nova Scotia via Panama and Mexico, hugging the coast to avoid a long stretch over open sea.

⊙ Migratory birds usually gather in flocks before beginning their journey. Birds on a wire are a sure sign of summer's end.

BIRD WATCHING

You can predict the weather by watching the way birds fly. "If the lark flies high, expect fair weather." "When swallows fleet soar high and sport in the air, the weather will be clear." In good weather, high air pressure and warm thermal currents take birds up high, and the higher they fly, the less pressure they find, which means easy high flying. In stormy weather air pressure lowers, so lower flying is less effort. Birds also fly closer than usual to the ground when the weather is getting damp in order to catch insects, which are unable to rise high with damp wings. "The low flight of rooks indicates rain." "Birds flying low, expect rain and a blow."

If you see migrating birds flying low, you can be quite sure of bad weather approaching. For successful migration birds need strong tail wind, and in fine, calm weather there is no headwind, so they can fly high. If a storm is brewing, the winds change as well as air pressure and birds have to drop down very low.

STRANGE BEHAVIOR

Sailors once used the behavior of seabirds to foretell the weather. Birds roost more during low pressure than high pressure, and in really low pressure huge flocks will often be seen waiting to rest out a storm. "Seabirds sit on the sand, it's a sign of rain when you're at hand."

Birds are often seen to wash before wet weather – "If fowls roll in the sand, rain is at hand," and they often make more noise. "When the peacock loudly bawls, then we'll have both rain and squalls." "When parrots whistle, expect rain." The green woodpecker is sometimes called the "rainbird" because he always calls before rain. Perhaps birds call because they know their usual calls will soon be drowned out; perhaps as a navigational aid – "When the goose honks low, expect foul weather" – perhaps to warn others to prepare to shelter. These sayings may also reflect the way sound is magnified before a storm when the pressure drops and the number of water droplets in the air increases.

If geese fly low enough for you to see their markings clearly, bad weather is on the way. If they are also honking loudly, a storm will soon follow.

LONG-RANGE PREDICTIONS

The cuckoo is a foreteller of spring in England, traditionally heard by the beginning of April. Its call is a timely reminder to plant potatoes. "When you hear the cuckoo shout, 'tis time to plant our tatties out." But if cuckoos sing after St. John's Day (June 24) the harvest will be late, as it will have been a late spring. "Cuckoo oats and woodcock hay makes the farmer run away." If the cuckoo calls during oat sowing, the farmer is sowing too late, and if woodcock are in the hay this means the same: a poor late harvest.

"One swallow does not make a summer" is a traditional saying, warning against hastily assuming summer has arrived.

SWALLOW

Animals

SINCE EARLIEST TIMES,

OBSERVATION OF ANIMAL

BEHAVIOR HAS BEEN

CONSIDERED A DEPENDABLE

METHOD OF INTERPRETING

THE WEATHER.

MYTH BUSTER

If you want to know the temperature, ask a cricket! They chirp at a rate that increases as the air temperature rises, so the higher the temperature, the greater number of chirps per minute. Count the number of chirps they make in fourteen seconds. That will be the temperature in their location. Or use the katydid's song as a rough guide:

Kate 58F
Kate-tee 62F
Kate-didn't 66F
Kay-tee-did 70F
Kay-tee-didn't 74F
Kay-tee-did it 78F

FARMYARD SIGNS

The idea that "pigs gather leaves and straw before a storm" is widespread countrylore, based on the observation that pigs sometimes went to their pens without finishing all their food when rain was coming. The notion that cows lie down before rain is also ancient weatherlore, accurate at least 75 percent of the time, since cows' undersides are not rainproof like their hides, so they need to keep as dry as possible. Cows in barns are reluctant to go out to pasture before a storm. Horses become restless. Dogs are said to spend more time asleep. Sheep become more active before a storm, and also eat more greedily than usual.

DEW ON A SPIDER'S WEB

Spiders are reliable indicators of changes in humidity. They only weave when the air is dry, so when you see them spinning you can be sure of fine weather.

"When spiders webs in air do fly, the spell will soon be very dry." Conversely "If garden spiders forsake their webs, it indicates rain."

CRICKET

TIP

"When locusts are heard, frost in six weeks" is a reliable southern U.S. warning to gardeners to think about winter preparations.

LONG-RANGE RELIABILITY

Many long-range weather predictions rely on the thickness of animals' coats, such as "If hair on bears and horses is thick early in season, expect a bad winter." It is hard to see how this could be rooted in fact, but hair is a good short-term indicator. As relative humidity increases, hair length and breadth expands by two and a half percent. So changes in hair can indicate that a storm is on the way.

Worms can sense approaching weather: "deep worms, frozen winter." They burrow deep when hard frosts are on the way, as frosts make moving through the top layers of soil difficult. This might also be to avoid predators, such as moles, that store large quantities of half-killed worms to see them through a cold spell.

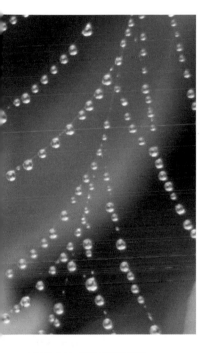

GROUNDHOG DAY

In northern Europe, February 2 or Candlemas Day has been an important forecasting date for centuries. If the sun appeared that day, six more weeks of cold weather were predicted, but if the weather was dull, summer would begin sooner. Early German settlers in Pennsylvania watched a groundhog (woodchuck). If he peeped out of his winter quarters on February 2 and saw his shadow, he went back into his burrow for another six weeks' nap; but on a cloudy day he would remain outside, indicating moderate weather to come. In the 19th century, Candlemas Day was renamed Groundhog Day: "If the sun shines on Groundhog Day; half the fuel and half the hay." However, the groundhog has only been right 39 percent of the time since records began in 1880!

GROUNDHOG

DONKEY

MYTH BUSTER

"When the ass begins to bray, be sure we shall have rain that day." Widely quoted, this 20th century folklore aphorism arose when a detachment of military weathermen in Italy lost all their instruments when a shell demolished their jeep. They came across a donkey that had the habit of braying for a long time when rain was on the way, so they used it to predict the weather, continuing to send forecasts to headquarters. All went well until a female donkey came along one day; after that the braying took on a different meaning.

COUNTRYFOLK LEARNED
TO TELL THE WEATHER,
THE TIME OF DAY, AND
PERHAPS THE COMPASS
POINTS FROM THE
FLOWERS AROUND THEM.
THIS KNOWLEDGE REMAINS
FASCINATING TODAY.

Weather & clock flowers

In one way or another, all plants respond to weather conditions. The response can be as simple as growing best in full sun, partial shade, or full shade. Or it can be more complicated.

WEATHER PLANTS

"Pimpernel, pimpernel, tell me true, whether the weather be fine or no." The scarlet pimpernel or poor man's weather-glass (*Anagallis arvensis*) closes or folds its leaves before rain, as does wild indigo (*Baptisia tinctoria*). The windflower (*Anemone nemorosa*) closes its petals and droops, and the fragrant common heliotrope (*Heliotropium arborescens*) won't open if rain is coming. Daisies (*Bellis* spp.) close up entirely before rain.

Lilac (*Syringa vulgaris*) blossoms are quicker to open in the morning when rain's on the way and slower when the air is dry. If the African marigold (*Tagetes erecta*) hasn't opened its petals by 8:00 a.m. it's said that it will rain or thunder that morning. Crocus (*Crocus* spp.), and tulips (*Tulipa* spp.), open their blossoms when the temperature rises, closing again when it falls.

SUNFLOWER

MYTH BUSTER

"When leaves show their undersides, be very sure that rain betides." Leaves tremble more when damp air softens the leaf stalks, so it is valid to assume that unsteady leaves on a still day mean rain is coming.

FOLLOW THE SUN

Sunflowers (*Helianthus annuus*) prefer to grow in full sun, their heads turning to follow the east-west path of the sun during the day, offering some clue to direction. The compass plant (*Silphium lactinianum*) is supposed to provide more accurate directional guidance. Its leaves are said to radiate from the stem in north and south directions, apparently so the warm sun dries them out less. But don't rely on this; it also depends on whether the plant is growing in sun or shade.

CLOCK PLANTS

MORNING GLORY

Scarlet pimpernel is also known as shepherd's-clock and shepherd's-calendar. Its scarlet flowers open at about 8 a.m. and close at about 3 p.m. The pale blue flowers of wild chicory *(Cichorium intybus)* once told English farm laborers the time, opening at 7 a.m. and closing at noon. Star-of-Bethlehem *(Ornithogalum umbellatum)* is often known as ten o'clock lady or nap at noon. Its white star flowers only open on bright days around 10 a.m. and shut at noon. Goatsbeard *(Tragopogon pratensis)* also closes its flowers at noon, hence its common name of Jack-go-to-bed-at-noon. Morning glory *(Ipomoea spp.)* is another clock plant. Its full flowering glory must be seen on a bright morning, the flowers are closed by mid-afternoon.

Some flowers are very late risers and will not bloom when the sun is still high in the sky. Four o'clocks *(Mirabilis jalapa)* and evening primrose *(Oenothera spp.)* avoid bright sunlight, preferring to flower in the evening. Many scented plants including jasmine *(Jasminum officinale)*, flowering tobacco *(Nicotiana alata)*, and annual stocks *(Matthiola incana)* are at their most fragrant in the evenings to attract specific night-flying pollinators.

TIP

Clock flowers are not always entirely accurate. For example, four o'clocks bloom in the late afternoon and are open throughout the night. They may not open exactly at 4 p.m. and they can open in the morning on cloudy days as the clouds fool them into thinking it's later in the afternoon.

 If you would like to devise a flower clock, see if some of the following are accurate in your area.

NATURE'S TIMING

"When the dogwood flowers appear, frosts will not again be here" is a traditional forecast. In the United Kingdom, blackthorn *(Prunus spinosa)* rather than dogwood *(Cornus* spp.) is the marker plant. Its blooming time varies according to air temperature and humidity: following a frosty spring, it will blossom up to two weeks later than in a mild year. Once it is in blossom sowing and planting can start.

OUR GARDENS ARE TUNED INTO THE NATURAL TURNING OF THE SEASONS. LEARN TO UNDERSTAND THE CLUES YOUR PLANTS PROVIDE ABOUT APPROACHING CONDITIONS.

Seasonal changes

FALL LEAF

DON'T BE HASTY

"Ne'er cast a clout till May be out" refers to May or hawthorn blossom *(Crataegus* spp.*)*; a clout is an article of clothing. A similar warning from Iowa relied on keeping winter clothes until the blooming of the blue flags *(Iris versicolor)*. Azaleas *(Rhododendron* spp.*)* draw in their leaves as temperatures drop so "When the wild azalea shuts its doors, that's when winter's tempest roars."

AZALEA

FUTURE PREDICTIONS

Some plants seem to know what the future holds. "As high as the weeds grow, so will the bank of snow" is a very reliable old saying. Before a hard winter, weeds grow taller than the deepest snow will be. Countryfolk say this is so snowbirds that feed on the weeds' seeds will not starve when snow covers all else. "Onion skin very thin, mild winter coming in. Onion skin thick and tough, coming winter cold and rough" is also often reliable, and a hard winter is forecast if corn husks are thick and tight, or apple skins are tough. Corn is also very sensitive to changes in air pressure. "If heads are dry and crisp, fine weather's here to stay; if heads droop damply down, then rain is on the way."

MYTH BUSTER

Plants cannot know the time of year at any given time, but they can work it out by measuring the length of night time. This is called photoperiodism, as shown in the color changes of poinsettia *(Euphorbia pulcherrima)*. Temperature also plays a part in flowering time. Spring-flowering bulbs produce flowers after a period of cold. And plants flower when the creatures that pollinate them are present.

LEAVES CHANGING COLOR

SEASONAL LEAF COLOR

The American writer Henry Thoreau used the color of the dogbane to indicate the onset of winter: "birdsongs lessen after the dogbane *(Apocynum androsaemifolium)* leaves turned yellow in autumn." The change in leaf color on the trees is one of the most notable indicators that the natural world is moving on. The green chlorophyll that triggers the food-making process of photosynthesis disappears from the leaves, as trees prepare to live off the food they have stored during the summer.

Just as squirrels store more nuts before a long winter, country-folk believe that trees lose their leaves later before a hard winter, as they are busy storing more food. "When leaves fall early, fall and winter will be mild; when leaves fall late, winter will be severe."

Fruits

The change of leaf color is a signal to preserve your fruits. Small fruits (blackberries and loganberries) are ideally suited to freezing. Apples and pears can be frozen (as slices rolled in sugar, poached in a light syrup, or as puree), or dried, or sliced. If you have a bumper crop you may be able to preserve some by each method.

Freezing

This is the most popular way of preserving fruits and vegetables, although some may loose their texture. You can avoid this by making fruit purees to freeze. Blanch vegetables, then lay them on open trays so they freeze separately.

You can also chop herbs into ice-cube trays, add water, then freeze.

Jellies and Jams

Do not use over-ripe or bruised fruits. Currants, damsons, and gooseberries have high pectin content and will form firm jams. For other fruits you will need to add pectin.

Jellies are similar to jams, except without the fruit pieces. Cook to setting point, place the fruit in a jelly bag and allow the liquid to drip off into a bowl.

Drying

Pick herbs, rinse, and pat dry. Place them on kitchen paper and bake in the oven (coolest setting, 1 hour). When dry, crumble into jars, and seal.

SELECTION OF OLD WEATHERLORE SAYINGS BY SEASON

Spring

All the months of the year, curse a fair Februeer.
If you have a warm, dry February, it means pests and diseases will be rife, as they will get a hold early rather than being killed by cold weather. As it's dry, there will be insufficient frost and moisture to break down the soil. It also means early blossoming of fruit trees, which will then be caught by later frosts and produce no fruit.

A good March comes in like a lion, goes out like a lamb.
Ideally, March should come in fiercely, with stormy weather, to prepare the ground for a productive spring.

April wet, good wheat.
Seedlings need rain in April.

Oak before ash, splash. Ash before oak, soak.
This old English saying remains constantly popular, yet the oak is always in leaf before the ash!

Summer

Shear your sheep in May, and shear them all away is a warning not to count on the weather too soon.

A wet May makes a big load of hay.
A cold May is kindly and fills the barn finely.
Young crops need plenty of watering in May, and a cold May means less pest and disease problems and stronger growth rather than flowering too soon.

A swarm of bees in May is worth a load of hay.
A swarm of bees in June is worth a silver spoon.
A swarm of bees in July is not worth a fly.

Mist in May and heat in June will bring all things into tune.
The ideal weather conditions: wet growing conditions and hot flowering.

St. Swithin's Day: if it does rain for forty days it will remain.
St. Swithin's Day: if it be fair for forty days will rain no more.
St. Swithin's Day is July 15. The myth is that when the new Winchester Cathedral was completed in 870 in England, St. Swithin's bones were moved. He "wept" so strongly that rain on this day is often followed by rain for forty days. In Italy, July 15 is St. Gallo's Day and the same forecast is predicted – often accurately.

If the first week in August is unusually warm, the coming winter will be white and long.

If a cold August follows a hot July, it foretells a winter hard and dry.

Dry August and warm does harvest no harm.

Fall

Heavy September rains bring drought.

September dries up wells or breaks down bridges.

In October dung your field and your land its wealth will yield.

Dry your barley in October or you'll always be sober.
If this is not done, there'll be no malt for beer.

If October bring much frost and wind, then are January and February mild.

Winter

On first of November if weather be clear, an end to the sowing you do for the year.
This is sound advice. Finish planting hardy vegetables and onions and garlic now.

If the first snowfall lands on unfrozen ground, the winter will be mild.

If ice will bear a man before Christmas, it will not bear a mouse afterward.

A January spring is worth nothing.
Beware when the weather looks too clear too soon; it is unlikely to last.

If you see grass in January, lock your grain in the granary.

CHAPTER 2

DOWN TO EARTH

TO BE A GOOD GARDENER, YOU NEED TO BE AN OPTIMIST AND AN ENTHUSIAST. BUT FIRST AND FOREMOST YOU NEED TO UNDERSTAND SOIL SO THAT YOU CAN WORK WITH NATURE TO GIVE A GARDEN WHAT IT NEEDS AND MAKE LIFE EASY FOR YOURSELF AND FOR YOUR PLANTS.

IF YOU ARE EVER FORTUNATE ENOUGH TO TAKE OVER A GARDEN THAT HAS BEEN TENDED BY A GARDENER FOR YEARS, YOU'LL FIND THAT YOU CAN GROW ANYTHING. IT'S NOTHING TO DO WITH GREEN THUMBS (OR FINGERS) AND ALL TO DO WITH IMPROVING THE CONDITION OF THE SOIL. YOU GET OUT OF GARDENING JUST WHAT YOU PUT IN, AND THE MOST IMPORTANT PART OF ANY GARDEN IS THE SOIL. START BY PAYING ATTENTION TO THIS VITAL FOUNDATION.

IF YOU FOLLOW IN THE FOOTSTEPS
OF TRADITIONAL GARDENERS, YOU CAN
TRANSFORM A BARE PLOT INTO A LUSH
PARADISE. START WITH THE BASICS AND
GET TO UNDERSTAND YOUR SOIL.

Soil basics

The biggest difference between humans and trees is not that we
walk about and they don't. It's that plants feed directly from soil.

ROOT CARE

"A frozen soil and a rocky bed make no good for beast nor
bread." Plants get their food, air, and water through their roots,
which need to spread to find what they need. Ideal soil should
include lots of air and water spaces, be firm enough so nutrients don't drain away, and crumbly enough for roots to access.
It mustn't bake too hard when it's sunny, nor hold puddles of
water after rain; it should warm up quickly but be slow to freeze.

**Rich, dark, crumbly soil is
the foundation of every
flourishing garden.**

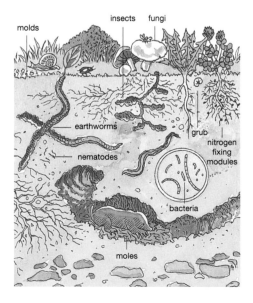

**Beneath the
soil's surface,
small animals,
insects, and
tiny organisms
transform decay-
ing matter and
soil minerals into
food for them-
selves and plants.**

FERTILE SOIL

Soil must be fertile, with a balance of organic matter and mineral
elements. Organic matter is the decaying remains of plant and
animal life, transformed by living organisms such as bacteria,
fungi, insects, and worms. Minerals result from the breakdown of
the underlying rocks, which are dissolved in the water in the soil.

MYTH BUSTER

Worms are your friends. They aerate the soil,
clear away and break down decaying plant
matter, and help soil fertility and drainage.
The common earthworm (Lumbricus terres-
tris) was taken to the U.S. by early colonists.
One worm can shift 30 tons of soil a year!

NUTRIENTS AND PH

Plants need a good supply of carbon, hydrogen, and oxygen, plus other elements. Sometimes known as the "major" nutrients, plants need nitrogen (N), phosphorus (P), and potassium (K), plus calcium, magnesium, and sulfur. They also need very small amounts of the "micronutrients" iron, manganese, copper, zinc, boron, and molybdenum. In a balanced soil that is well drained and full of organic matter, plants will be able to get at all these elements without extra help.

Even if your soil is full of nutrients, plants may have difficulty absorbing nutrition if the pH is wrong; a pH scale shows how acid or alkaline soil is; whether it contains too little or too much lime. The lime content can affect all the other elements in your soil, so it is important to get it right.

Buy a simple pH testing kit from a garden store. The neutral point on the pH scale is 7; soils below that become increasingly acid (too little lime) and above 7 are increasingly alkaline (too much lime). The most fertile soil is very slightly acid, around pH 6.5. Add lime to acid soils according to package instructions; add compost to soils with too much lime.

TIP

Gardeners sometimes make a simple taste test to check to see if soil is acid. Acid soil smells and tastes sour. It's more reliable to drop a piece of soil into a jar of vinegar. If the vinegar starts to bubble, your soil has plenty of lime. If there are no bubbles, lime the soil with 4 oz (100 g) lime to the square yard (meter).

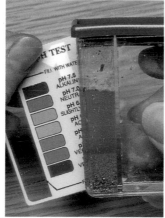

○ Buy a special pH tester from your garden store to check the pH level of your soil and to find out which nutrients your soil needs. Take a sample of soil, mix it with water, and transfer the solution to the tester. Add the capsule supplied and match the color of your sample to the scale on the tester.

MYTH BUSTER

Many popular garden plants including azaleas *(Rhododendron* spp.*)*, camellias *(Camellia* spp.*)*, gardenias *(Gardenia* spp.*)*, and cardinal flower *(Lobelia cardinalis)* prefer more acid soil (pH below 6.5). If your soil is too alkaline, you should grow them in containers or raised beds in special soil. If you can't resist them in your borders, water the plants with dilute vinegar – 4 tablespoons of vinegar per pint (½ liter) – once a month during the growing season. Or follow the old advice of adding coffee grounds to the soil; their slight acidity takes the edge off an alkaline environment.

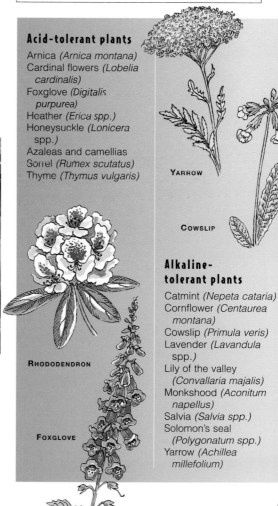

Acid-tolerant plants

Arnica *(Arnica montana)*
Cardinal flowers *(Lobelia cardinalis)*
Foxglove *(Digitalis purpurea)*
Heather *(Erica* spp.*)*
Honeysuckle *(Lonicera* spp.*)*
Azaleas and camellias
Sorrel *(Rumex scutatus)*
Thyme *(Thymus vulgaris)*

YARROW

COWSLIP

Alkaline-tolerant plants

Catmint *(Nepeta cataria)*
Cornflower *(Centaurea montana)*
Cowslip *(Primula veris)*
Lavender *(Lavandula* spp.*)*
Lily of the valley *(Convallaria majalis)*
Monkshood *(Aconitum napellus)*
Salvia *(Salvia* spp.*)*
Solomon's seal *(Polygonatum* spp.*)*
Yarrow *(Achillea millefolium)*

RHODODENDRON

FOXGLOVE

BEFORE YOU EVEN GET OUT A SPADE TO TURN OVER
YOUR SOIL, TAKE A LOOK AT WHAT'S GROWING IN
YOUR YARD AND HOW HEALTHY THE PLANTS LOOK.

Looking at soil

IDENTIFY YOUR SOIL

You're unlikely to want a yard full of weeds and wild plants, but don't feel compelled to till them out until you've identified them. They can tell you what's going on below the surface and the type of soil you're dealing with.

"Gold under thistle, silver under rushes, famine under heath."

This old saying gives you some idea of the type of soil different plants grow in. Thistles grow in rich fertile soil, rushes need reasonable fertility to flourish, but heathers grow in very acid soil that's inhospitable to most plants.

Take a good look at the condition of your soil before deciding on your course of action.

MYTH BUSTER

"Nettles today, fruit tomorrow." Few people want a yard full of nettles. But nettles like a rich, damp soil and they send their creeping roots out deep into the soil to mine for minerals, so when you pull them up you are left with mineral-rich soil ready to supply your plants with the elements they need. As the old saying suggests, nettle-fertilized soil is particularly good for soft-fruit bushes. Or, if you leave a few in the ground, they stimulate the growth of plants nearby and make them more resistant to diseases.

NETTLE

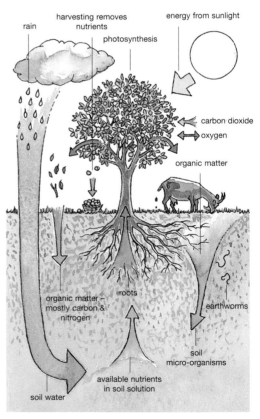

rain

harvesting removes nutrients

photosynthesis

energy from sunlight

carbon dioxide

oxygen

organic matter

organic matter – mostly carbon & nitrogen

roots

earthworms

soil micro-organisms

available nutrients in soil solution

soil water

Some plants, including nettles, mine deep into the subsoil for minerals. They bring them nearer the surface, so nearby plants can benefit.

HUNGRY PLANTS

If some plant nutrients are lacking in the soil, then the plants that are most successful at seeking them out will flourish. If your soil is lacking in nitrogen, plants that fix it from the air will be evident. These are typically members of the pea family, including clover *(Trifolium pratense)*, black medic *(Medicago lupulina)*, and wild lupines *(Lupinus angustifolius)*.

CARDINAL FLOWER

Plants that indicate poorly drained soil

Cattails *(Typha* spp.*)*
Horsetails *(Equisetum* spp.*)*
Joe-Pye weed *(Eupatorium purpureum)*
Ragged robin *(Lychnis floscuculi)*
Sedges *(Carex* spp.*)*
Cardinal flower*(Lobelia cardinalis)*
Silverweed *(Potentilla anserina)*
Coltsfoot *(Tussilago farfara)*
Bog pimpernel *(Anagallis tenella)*

INDICATOR PLANTS

"Sorrel stores strife." Some weeds thrive in soils that are rather acid. Groups of sorrel plants *(Rumex* spp.*)* suggest a lack of lime in the soil, therefore low fertility. If you have carnivorous plants you definitely have a problem soil, as they will only flourish in really acid soils where their roots cannot get the proteins they need from the soil, so they have to resort to catching flies and other insects for food.

If, on the other hand, your yard is boasting a fine crop of healthy looking dandelion *(Taraxacum officinale)*, wild mustard *(Brassica nigra)*, and pigweed *(Amaran-thus* spp.*)*, you should feel confident about the balance of your soil. These weeds will only grow well in fertile soils.

The most reliable indicator plants are the ones that like poorly drained soil. If you only have one or two types, or they're not flourishing, don't worry. But, if you have a whole collection, you know you'll need to improve the drainage to make a healthy garden. Moss and fungi on the ground also suggest that you may have a drainage problem.

JOE-PYE WEED

Types of soil

TROWEL AND SOIL

YOU CAN MAKE
ANY SOIL FERTILE
AND PRODUCTIVE,
BUT KNOWING WHAT
YOU START OFF WITH
WILL MAKE THE JOB
OF TENDING YOUR
PLANTS MUCH EASIER.

An old saying suggests that soil should be "light enough to root, firm enough to stay," meaning it should have plenty of spaces for the roots to delve down and get air and water, but solid enough to store the elements they need for food.

GROUND RULES

Before you worry about what type of soil you're dealing with, find out how easy the soil is to break up and work, and how rich it is likely to be. You can tell a great deal by looking at your soil's color and texture, putting a fork into it, and holding some in your hand. Is it heavy and difficult to dig? Is it dark and rich, or light and sandy? Dark soil should contain plenty of the organic matter necessary for successful gardening. Light-colored soil will be lower in nutrients. Heavy soil will get waterlogged easily and will need breaking up.

Whatever soil you start with, add organic matter to transform even a poor patch of ground into a lush and productive garden.

SOIL CATEGORIES

Anyone who works the soil soon gets to know how it behaves. 18th century gardeners advised to "Plant later in sand or plant once more after spring rains," knowing that floods could wash seeds as well as nutrients from sandy soil. Many old country sayings advise when to plant different crops in clay. It is useful to categorize your soil as a way of helping find the best way to garden.

Put a sample of soil into a screw-top jar, add water, shake well, and let settle. Clay soil will have a thin layer of gritty water topped by thick soil. Sandy soil will have a thin layer of soil above a broad band of gritty water.

WAYS OF TESTING

A simple hand test is one good way to find out more about your soil. Pick up a small handful and roll it between your fingers. Try to roll it into a ball. If it won't stick together, it is probably light sandy soil. If it feels rather gritty but forms a ball, you are probably holding loam. If it is sticky and you can make the surface shine when you rub your thumb over it, you have a handful of clay.

Clay soils

Clay soils consist of tiny mineral particles that stick together very easily rather than forming crumbs. They are very sticky with few spaces in between the particles for air or for water to drain away. Although they store nutrients well, it can be hard for plant roots to get at them. They are heavy to work, tend to get waterlogged, and in a drought they dry into a hard cracked surface that water can't penetrate. Clay soils are good for deep-rooted plants, such as comfrey and mints, brassicas, peas, broad beans, potatoes, pears, and plums.

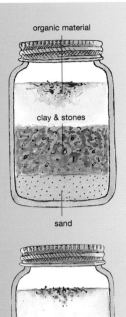

organic material

clay & stones

sand

Sandy soils

Sandy soils are described as light – they have masses of large particles that do not hold together well. This means that plant roots can easily get at air and water in the spaces between the crumbs but the soils drain very easily, so do not hold nutrients well. Sandy soils are good for many alpine and arid plants; herbs such as lavender, tarragon, and thyme; carrots and other root vegetables; onions and tomatoes.

Loam soils

Loam soils have a balanced mix of smaller and larger particles, so they store nutrients, offer satisfactory drainage, and are easy for the plant roots to access. Most garden plants grow well in loam.

OLD-FASHIONED GARDENERS WOULD BE AMAZED BY
THE RANGE OF ARTIFICIAL FERTILIZERS NOW WIDELY
AVAILABLE. FOLLOW THEIR EXAMPLE INSTEAD AND
USE CHEAP AND HEALTHY NATURAL FERTILIZERS.
YOUR PLANTS WILL THRIVE.

Soil improvement

⬤ Poultry manure is the best of all farmyard manures for your garden. It is particularly rich in nitrogen.
Use it sparingly, preferably well rotted with straw.

TIP

Farmyard manure, such as cow manure, can give off ammonia. If you use it fresh, your plants may be scorched. Instead, store it for six months to a year in a covered heap or in closed bags. This allows it to rot and any weed seeds will be killed as the pile heats. Dig well-rotted manure into the ground for vegetables or spread it among your ornamentals as a mulch or topdressing. Potatoes thrive on composted manure, but don't use it near carrots or other root vegetables, as the long roots will feed on the manure instead of going down into the soil.

TIP

If your soil is poor and has bad drainage, dig in compost in the fall and spring. Otherwise use it as a mulch on top of the ground where it will slowly seep into the soil, while keeping the ground moist and preventing weed growth.

ANIMAL MANURE

Adding aged manure to your soil makes it more fertile, helps lighten a heavy clay soil, and adds substance and moisture retention to a light, sandy one. "In October dung your field, and your land it's wealth will yield." Many traditional gardeners kept fowl and pigs and their manure was composted for several months, then dug into, or spread on, flower and vegetable beds. Horse droppings were collected and dried or composted and put on rosebeds. Bat droppings were used, and people living near the sea collected seaweed and bird droppings. These are all rich in the minerals your garden needs.

Peter Henderson's 19th Century manual *Gardening for Profit* recommends "pure Peruvian guano" for the market gardens of New York, as well as horn and whalebone scrapings from factory waste (bonemeal is a high-protein plant food).

GREEN MANURE

"Where banks be amended and newly upcast, sow mustardseed after a shower be past." Sometimes considered a new fad, the practice of planting crops for green manure has been around for centuries. Also called a cover crop, this living layer of plants adds nutrition to the soil as they grow by fixing nitrogen, or bringing minerals near the surface; then you dig them in, and they add more. Green manure crops also prevent weeds from colonizing empty beds, and can deter pests and diseases.

CLOVER

MUSTARD

Clovers (*Trifolium pratense* and *Melilotus* spp.) add nitrogen and also suppress weeds and add minerals. Mustard (*Brassica nigra*) grows fast in early spring or fall, it suppresses weeds, brings up minerals from deep within the soil, and makes them more available for a following crop. It also helps clear some soil pests. But don't let mustard go to seed or you'll be forever pulling it up from your garden.

TIP

Buy green manures by the pound from a farm-seed supplier; don't buy them in expensive fancy packets.

Natural fertilizers

Manure – well-aged strawy manure can be added any time. Cow and sheep manure can be used fresh dug into sandy soil in fall when the garden is resting for the winter. Only ever use well-rotted manure on heavy soils.
Compost – can be spread or dug in any time.
Seaweed – high in nutrients and unlocks micronutrients from soil. Use any time as a plant or soil pick-me-up.
Straw – good spring mulch for light soils. High in carbon content, so best combined with nitrogen-rich grass clippings.
Fall leaves – chop with mower; then store in sacks for a year before using as a mulch or digging them in.
Rock dust – powdered, solves some mineral deficiencies.
Peanut shells – carbon-rich, help to aerate compost piles.

FALL LEAVES

Making compost

FOLLOW THE EXAMPLE OF TRADITIONAL GARDENERS AND PUT ALL YOUR KITCHEN SCRAPS AND GARDEN WASTE INTO A COMPOST HEAP TO ROT INTO NUTRITIOUS COMPOST. IT MAKES A PERFECT – AND FREE – SOIL SUPPLEMENT; SOIL BECOMES FRIABLE, RETAINS MOISTURE, AND PROVIDES NUTRIENTS SLOWLY.

The composting process is simple. You throw away old kitchen scraps, old flowers, and garden rubbish, and a host of microscopic creatures turn this waste into something you can use in your garden.

You can make compost in a few weeks by combining a whole load of materials in different layers in a compost bin all at once, where it will heat up quickly and rot, as long as you turn the pile regularly. Or you can take your time, adding scraps and plant material as you have them and letting a heap slowly mature over a couple of seasons. Then use your compost as a mulch or dig it in to help improve soil structure, feed plants, and help control diseases.

MYTH BUSTER

In the 18th century it became popular practice to lay banana skins in the hole before planting roses, or place them in a trench under vegetables. They rot quickly and provide calcium, magnesium, sulfur, phosphates, sodium, and silica. They are also useful on a compost heap, helping to speed up the composting process.

BANANA

Transform kitchen and garden waste into rich compost – the ideal slow-release fertilizer for all your plants' needs.

WHAT CAN YOU COMPOST?

Grass cuttings, manure, and young weeds are all swift to compost. Mix them with fruit and vegetable scraps, tea bags and coffee grounds, egg shells, vegetable plant remains, old flowers, soft prunings, horse, rabbit or hamster bedding, perennial weeds that have been left in the sun to dry, and young hedge clippings.

MAINTAINING YOUR COMPOST HEAP

Composting needs air, moisture, and warmth. A traditional compost heap is just a heap of waste materials, which can take six to twelve months to produce rich, usable compost. It rots faster in summer.

Never let your compost dry out. Keep it moist by watering in dry weather, or the decomposition process will stop.

To keep it tidy, you could wrap wire mesh around four posts, or make a cheap bin from a bottomless plastic garbage can with holes pierced in the side. Or you can buy one. Enclosed bins keep the heat in and speed up the process, but a slower free-form pile works just as well in the long run.

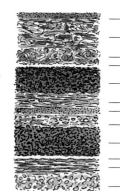

COMFREY

Wire cage bins keep compost well aired, but they may need insulating by wrapping cardboard or old carpet round them. Make sure a plastic bin holds at least 3 cubic ft (250 L), or your compost may never heat up.

Never compost meat or fish, cat litter or dog drop-pings, disposable napkins or glossy magazines. Don't put too many grass cuttings into your compost at once, or they get slimey. Add them in layers of approximately 4 in (10 cm), alter-nating with other materials.

topsoil
weeds
kitchen waste
fine lime
farmyard manure
grass cuttings
topsoil
crop residue
farmyard manure
fine lime
grass cuttings
soft hedge trimmings

WORM BINS

Ideal for apartment dwellers with a balcony or those with tiny yards, a worm bin contains worms (*Eisenia foetida*) that live on compost, shredded newspaper, and kitchen scraps. They eat the kitchen waste and turn it into worm castings, richer than other forms of compost. Worm bins must be kept warm in winter, so keep the bin indoors, but in summer you can put it outside.

43

IT SEEMS SIMPLE – TAKE A SPADE AND DIG THE SOIL. BUT TAKE THE TIME TO LEARN A FEW OLD TIPS FOR SUCCESSFUL CULTIVATION AND YOU COULD SAVE YOURSELF A LOT OF TIME AND TROUBLE.

Digging or leaving

MYTH BUSTER

You don't have to dig! You can practice no-digging. You will only need a spade to spread at least 2 in (5 cm) of well-rotted compost on the surface of your soil; keep the level up all the time and renew it from year to year. Just sow your seeds or plant your plants in that. That is all there is to it. The no-digging technique is low maintenance and high reward, but you do need to have access to a large supply of compost.

SPADE

WHEN TO WORK THE SOIL

"Till the soil on midsummer's day, not feast aye famine will come your way. Till the soil in April showers, you will have not fruit nor flowers."

Proverbs are rooted firmly in good practice, as no good gardener should work their soil when it is either very dry or very wet. If you dig when the soil is very dry, you risk loosening the crumbs too much and destroying its ability to hold water. But if you dig when the soil is very wet, you'll compact it and make it hard for the water to drain away. In either case, you make life harder for the plants and yourself.

On very hot days in England and America, gardeners used to start work at dawn, and finish at midday, returning early evening. If you need to plant in high summer, work in the early morning before the sun is high or when it has set, and water the ground well afterward. This gives soil and plants the maximum opportunity to recover. If you do plant in very wet weather, avoid treading on the soil that you are working. Stand on a broad board to spread the weight.

Whether you choose to dig or
not, your soil will reward you
handsomely if you treat it well.
Leave it alone in very wet or dry
weather, and add compost on fine
spring and fall days.

SIMPLE DOUBLE DIGGING

Step 1
Double digging
is the best way
of improving poor
soil. Divide your
plot into sections
about 1 ft (30
cm) wide.

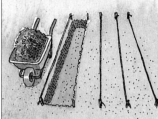

Step 2
Remove all the
topsoil from the
first section and
put it into a
wheelbarrow.

Step 3
Loosen the subsoil
by driving a fork
into the bottom of
your trench and
working it back
and forth.

Step 4
Fill the first trench
with topsoil from
the second sec-
tion, incorporating
some well-rotted
compost or man-
ure with it. The
topsoil from the
first trench will fill
your final section.

WORM SERVICE

Once a flower border is planted, you should never need to dig
it again. Leave that job to the worms. Just spread mulch or
compost on the surface in fall or spring. But if you need to
remove a plant or add a new one, dig a hole more than twice
the size of the container or rootball of the plant, add some
compost to the planting hole, and mix the soil with more as
you backfill the hole.

ROTOTILLING

If you have a fair-sized garden you may decide to use a rototiller to prepare the ground. This is a speedy way of digging,
weeding, and loosening soil, and can be used as a way of
incorporating compost or green manure. But try not to get too
carried away as overuse of a rototiller can actually make a weed
problem worse by chopping up small bits of creeping rootlet
and distributing them far and wide, and excessive cultivation
will destroy your crumbly soil texture and make for a compacted
hard-to-work soil. Instead, use it to prepare new beds, or once
a year to loosen soil before planting.

CHAPTER 3

MAKING A START

NOWADAYS WE CAN BUY ANY PLANT WE DESIRE FROM GARDEN CENTERS AND SPECIALIST NURSERIES; THE WORLD OF PLANTS IS LITERALLY AT OUR FINGER-TIPS THROUGH THE WORLD-WIDE WEB. BUT SPARE A THOUGHT FOR EARLIER GARDENERS WHOSE GARDENS WERE SHAPED IN A VERY DIFFERENT WAY. SOME PLANTS WERE INVITED INTO GARDENS OUT OF THE WILD; OTHERS CAME FROM FRIENDS, NEIGHBORS, OR OTHER GARDENERS.

SEEDS WERE SAVED DILIGENTLY FOR REPLANT-ING THE NEXT YEAR, AND CUTTINGS WERE BEGGED, BARTERED FOR, OR TAKEN SURREPTITIOUSLY. GREAT CARE WAS TAKEN IN PROPAGATION AND CULTI-VATION, BECAUSE IT WAS NOT ALWAYS EASY TO ACQUIRE MORE PLANTS. WE CAN LEARN A GREAT DEAL FROM THESE OLD METHODS AND ENJOY THE PLEASURE OF RAISING COVETED SPECIMENS FROM FRIENDS' GARDENS RATHER THAN BUYING THEM.

BEFORE THERE WERE SEED MERCHANTS AND PLANT STORES, PLANTS SPREAD THROUGH SHARING. PLANT PROPAGATION IS NOT AN EXACT SCIENCE BUT THE BASICS ARE SIMPLE.

Spreading treasures

PINKS

Many of our favorite garden flowers, including pinks (*Dianthus* spp.), lavender (*Lavandula* spp.), pot marigolds (*Calendula officinalis*), morning glories (*Ipomoea* spp.), hollyhocks (*Althea rosea*), and hundreds of others have spread around the world from the earliest gardens.

PLANT TERMS

Annuals are plants that bloom, set seed, and die – all in one growing season and have to be sown every year. The Latin name often gives you a clue: for example, the sunflower (*Helianthus annuus*) or stocks (*Matthiola incana*). Annuals are usually tender; that means they will not withstand cold, frosty weather, but they are easy to grow; simply sow the seeds in spring and enjoy the rewards.

Perennials survive as living roots from year to year. Some, including daylilies (*Hemerocallis* spp.), are extremely long-lived, while others, including lavender (*Lavandula* spp.), can die suddenly for no apparent reason after only a few years. The best way to propagate most perennials is by taking cuttings or dividing clumps, but you can try sowing seeds, too.

Biennials blossom during their second year and die back shortly after setting seeds. However, their seeds are usually hardy and they often self-seed or send up plantlets from the original plant. Foxgloves (*Digitalis* spp.) and hollyhocks (*Althea rosea*) are biennial. It is easiest to let biennials increase their own stock by self-sowing, then transplant the new seedlings where you want them in spring.

FOXGLOVES

OLD AND NEW VARIETIES

Most old-fashioned garden flowers are open-pollinated, which means they will come true from seeds, or look like the parent plant. Hybrids are created when plants from two different families are crossed to make a flower with a particular color or habit. Many hybrid plants have very exciting colors and shapes. Offspring of hybrids will revert to the strongest characteristics in their breeding. This is why glorious brightly colored ruffled flowers of hybrid columbine (*Aquilegia hybrida)* that self-sow often revert to plain murky purple. To raise hybrid offspring, take cuttings or divide plants when they are large enough.

PLANT DEVELOPMENT

Ever since the first gardener saved the seeds of a particular color of flower to try to reproduce it the following year, humans have tried to control plant development. People labor long and hard to produce the largest, brightest, and best shaped pest-, weather-, and disease-resistant varieties. The Shirley poppy is a very good example of a plant bred from traditional red cornfield poppies (*Papaver rhoeas).*

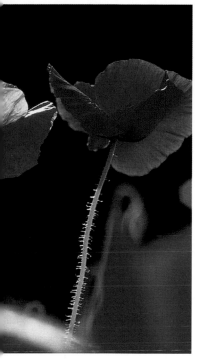

Red poppies, as above, are often found in cornfields. In 1881, the Reverend Wilkes of Shirley, England, found a scarlet poppy with a white rim in a field by his churchyard. He saved seeds from it and, over a few years, bred a new poppy – the Shirley poppy – with reliably white-edged petals.

GENETIC ENGINEERING

Genetically engineered seeds were first developed to produce plants that are resistant to diseases, or that tolerate herbicides. These seeds are produced by gene splicing, where a person mechanically moves DNA from one cell to another. Thinking about this process makes some people uncomfortable, because it raises the possibility that traits can be moved from dissimilar organisms, between animals and plants for example.

There is fierce debate about the pros and cons of genetic engineering (GE). Environmental arguments center on whether GE crops can pollute other species through pollination; whether it is wise to make crops resistant to herbicides because this promotes the use of herbicides and will lead eventually to weeds also becoming herbicide resistant; and questions about how other plants and wildlife will have to adapt. Moral arguments look at questions of individual growers' and consumers' rights, and whether a few huge companies can have the right to control the supply of seeds.

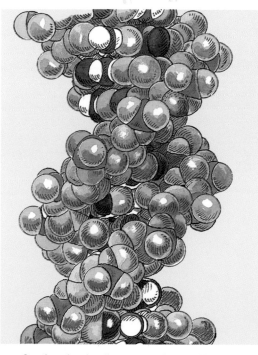

Genetic engineering allows genes to be moved from animals to plants, as well as between different species of plants. GE crops could solve future food shortages, but there are many environmental and ethical questions.

Saving seeds

YOU CAN GET NEARLY
EVERY KIND OF PLANT
FROM A BRIGHTLY
COLORED SEED PACKET,
BUT THERE IS A SPECIAL
PLEASURE IN SAVING
YOUR OWN SEEDS.

A FAIR EXCHANGE

"Good huswives in summer will save their own seeds against the next year, as occasion needs: one seed for another, to make an exchange, with fellowly neighborhood, seemeth not strange." This 16th-century adage summed up centuries of tradition. For thousands of years all farmers and gardeners had to save their seeds in order to have new crops the next year.

"Pluck not the flower if you cherish the seed." A proportion of every crop used to be left unpicked to mature to seeds. Nowadays you can buy nearly any kind of seeds you want. But it is satisfying to grow new plants from your own seeds. It is also important to save seeds to preserve old varieties of plants so they don't get lost forever in favor of currently fashionable hybrid varieties.

Store seeds in a cool, dry container, but make sure they are clearly labeled.

TIP

Ripe seeds should be saved from dry plants. It is best to collect them in midmorning after any dew has evaporated. If wet weather sets in, pull the whole plant from the ground when seed heads or pods are ripe, and hang it somewhere dry and airy until it is ready to harvest.

COLLECTING SEEDS

Always collect seeds on a dry day, before the seed heads pop open and scatter the seeds far and wide. Most seeds, such as beans and peas, are easy to save – just leave some pods unharvested on the bushes to dry until the peas rattle in the pods. Then take the seeds from the pods and store them in an airtight container in a cool dry place. Gardeners used to store larger seeds in sealed glass jars, and smaller seeds in brown paper packets. Don't use plastic or your seeds may get moldy.

Leave a proportion of your bean crop unpicked, so that the seeds can ripen. Harvest the seeds once the pods have dried and store them in an airtight container in a cool, dry place.

To be sure of collecting seeds before they drop, tie paper bags around the heads of small seeded plants a week or two before the seeds ripen.

Separate seeds from stems, old petals, and husks, by tossing them in a flat basket or sieve.

TIP

• To save the seeds of pulpy fruits and vegetables, scoop out the seeds and separate them from the pulp. Leave seeds to dry for several days in a cool, airy place before storing.

• Love-lies-bleeding or Joseph's coat is the most popular amaranth (*Amaranthus spp.*) today. The plants were once vital food stuff. The heads of these and many other heavily laden, small-seeded plants tend to drop their seeds so it is a good idea to tie a paper bag around the seed head for a week before collecting the seeds. It is good practice to do this for onions too.

OLD VARIETIES

Sweet peas of our youth always seemed to smell sweeter than the ones we grow today. That is not just nostalgia: modern varieties have been developed for the size of their petals and their colors rather than the scent. If you find some old-fashioned sweet peas, ask the grower if you can have some seeds, or buy them from a specialized supplier and save them from year to year. Because sweet peas are annuals, you must save the seeds every year once you find the scent you want.

DRY CLEANING

If you collect seeds after very dry weather, there's no need to take the seeds from the seed head immediately. Sweet peas and morning glory seeds can be stored happily in their pods. Poppy seed heads can be dried and stored whole. Other seeds should be separated from their chaff before storing in an airtight container in a cool, dry place. Simply place the seeds, with their bits of stem, old petals, husks and so on, in an old-fashioned sieve or flat basket and toss them slowly into the air. The chaff will blow away on a gentle breeze.

MYTH BUSTER

Seed savers are sometimes discouraged, believing storage is a problem – commercial seed packets come hermetically sealed, with the seeds often encased in foil. It is just as good to store seeds wrapped in plain paper, brown paper, or wax paper envelopes. Label them well and store them in a tin or a drawer in a dry, dark, cool place, preferably that has a constant temperature, or in the refrigerator. It is a good idea to write the date of collection on each packet, because seeds lose viability as they age.

SEEDLINGS

Seeds can be sown indoors in a huge variety of pots and seed trays.

Sowing seeds

THERE ARE MANY SAYINGS RELATING TO HOW AND WHEN TO SOW AND PLANT. THEY REFLECT PRACTICE THROUGH CENTURIES AND SHOULD NOT BE IGNORED.

MYTH BUSTER

Some gardeners try to give their plants a head start by sowing outdoors in the first warm days of spring, but it is soil rather than air temperature that controls seed germination. When to start depends on your soil and situation, but if you follow the old English saying you won't go far wrong: "If you can sit on the ground with your trousers down, then sow your seeds." Or don't try and sow your seeds when the ground is too cold, or you'll have little success.

TIMING

"Sow dry and plant wet." This golden rule is sound common sense. Wait for a spell of dry weather before sowing your seeds outdoors, and don't plant seeds in very wet conditions or you may lose many to mold and fungus. They don't want to be bone dry, or they will sit and do nothing, but they need to be given only enough moisture to coax them to germinate.

"First the farmer sows the seed, then he stands and takes his ease. Stamps his feet and claps his hand, and turns him round to view the land."

This 15th century rhyme reminds us of another rule of sowing: always firm the soil around the seeds, either by treading on it, or firming it with the back of your hand. If seeds are sown into a loose growing medium, cold, dry air can shrivel or dry them as they begin to germinate.

SOWING SEEDS

Outdoors, sow seeds into a bed of well-cultivated and finely raked soil. Indoors, sow seeds into a clean pot or seed tray containing sterile commercial seed starting mix, or use vermiculite or perlite mixed with good compost or soil. Fill the container to just below its rim and press the soil mix lightly around the edges to make sure that there are no air pockets.

Sow seeds thinly on the surface of the soil mix, or check instructions on your seed packet for sowing depth. Tap them directly from the seed packet or from a folded piece of paper. Begonias *(Begonia* spp.*)* and some other plants produce tiny, dust-like seeds, so mix their seeds with a small quantity of fine sand so you can distribute them more evenly. Large or pelleted seeds can be sown straight into individual pots.

A SIMPLE PROPAGATOR

Step 1
Fill a seed box with seed compost.

Step 2
Sprinkle small seeds on top and cover with finely sifted sand. If seeds are larger, cover with compost.

Step 3
Cover box with a sheet of glass and lay newspaper on top of the glass.

WATERING SEEDS

Water your seeds lightly as soon as they are sown by placing the trays in tepid water until the soil is moist – this doesn't disturb them. To maintain even humidity, you can cover trays or pots with a sheet of glass or clear plastic and, if seeds require darkness to germinate, place a sheet of newspaper on it until seeds begin to sprout. Keep your seed trays shaded and keep the soil mixture moist. When the first shoots emerge remove any covers.

Leave seedlings in the containers until they have at least three pairs of leaves. Then plant them into weed-free, crumbly soil, handling each one as little as possible. Do this in wet weather so the roots have the best chance of taking hold. Don't worry if they look sad for a few days – just keep them shaded and damp.

TIP

Cardboard egg cartons make excellent seed pots. Put one large seed or seedling into each egg compartment in the carton. When it's time to plant seedlings out, slice the egg carton into separate containers and plant each section into the ground without disturbing any roots. Toilet paper tubes are also good, as they will decompose into the soil.

Keep indoors until seedling is big enough to plant out

Cut off each cup and plant out

Cardboard egg cartons make environmentally friendly seedling pots

IN NATURE, PLANTS REPRODUCE NATURALLY; SEEDS FALL TO THE GROUND, GERMINATE, AND NEW PLANTS GROW. BUT GARDENERS HAVE TO GIVE SOME SEEDS A HELPING HAND.

PEPPER

Success with seeds

TOMATO

EGGPLANT

TIP

• Native Americans always sowed morning glory (*Ipomoea* spp.) seeds with melon seeds. Morning glories produce an enzyme that helps the melon seeds to germinate.

• If in doubt, don't bury seeds too deeply. Plants with thin coats need light for germination. Lettuce (*Laetuca sativa*), wildflowers, and love-in-a-mist (*Nigella damascena*) must be sown near the surface, so light will trigger germination. A few, typically larger, seeds require darkness, including Phlox (*Phlox* spp.).

Most annual flower and vegetable seeds need very little moisture and warmth to germinate. Wait until the soil temperature warms up and sow into finely raked soil or start seeds indoors in trays. Sun-loving vegetables like tomatoes and peppers germinate best with a little bottom heat. Place trays on top of the refrigerator or other warm place for a few days.

GARDEN SEEDS

Many garden species need cold and dampness to germinate, because in the wild seeds would remain dormant through the cold of winter and sprout in the spring. Their seeds contain compounds that ensure that the seeds remain dormant until the right conditions are met. Abcisic acid is produced in early fall so the seeds become dormant; during the cold of winter, enzymes in the seeds degrade the acid. Traditional practice was to bury the seeds in containers left outdoors to overwinter. It is easier to place seeds, such as clematis (*Clematis* spp.), in a sealed plastic bag containing a little slightly moist soil or vermiculite, and keep it in your refrigerator for at least four weeks. Then sow them in a warm place and they will assume that spring has come.

LOVE-IN-A-MIST

"On Candlemas Day sow beans in the clay."
This ancient wisdom is rooted in fact. The
first step in germination is for the seed to
soak up water, so it expands and breaks the
seed coat. In the Northern Hemisphere, on
Candlemas day (February 2) clay soil is still
cold and wet, so seeds will therefore be
surrounded by moisture to soften the hard
seed coating. Then, when the seeds are
ready to sprout, the ground is warming up.
If sowing later in the season, moisten seeds
of all members of the pea and bean family
by soaking them overnight in cold water
before planting.

TIP

• Sow sparsely into seed
trays. Overcrowding can
encourage damping off
fungus *(Sclerotina* spp.*)*
(see page 109), or your
seedlings may be weak.

• Sowing between 2:00 p.m.
and 4:00 p.m. gives a better
rate of germination than
sowing in the morning or
early evening. This is
because the temperature-
sensitive phase of the
germination process is
completed at night when
soil temperatures are lower.

Always soak sweet pea seeds *(Lathyrus odorata)* in water
overnight before sowing. Then they will virtually hit the
soil sprouting and will be up in a couple of days.

SCARIFICATION

Many seeds have a very hard coat, which cannot be easily
penetrated by water to start germination. In nature, the seeds
are eaten by birds; while traveling through a bird's digestion
and out, the seed coat is weakened enough to allow it to absorb
moisture when reaching the ground. Try rubbing the surface of
the seeds very gently between two sheets of sandpaper. Known
as scarification, this helps plants, such as milk vetch *(Astralagas*
spp.*)* and lupines *(Lupinus* spp.*)*, to germinate.

PARSLEY

To deter the devil, boiling
water used to be poured
over the ground before
sowing parsley. This
may have a basis in fact.
Parsley germination is
notoriously difficult, and
it seems to help to heat
the ground before sowing
the seeds.

EVERY GARDENER WANTS TO GIVE HIS OR HER
PLANTS AS MUCH OF A HEAD START AS POSSIBLE,
AND SAVE MONEY AT THE SAME TIME. SO IT IS
WORTH FOLLOWING SOME TRADITIONAL TIPS.

Plant seedlings in well-tilled crumbly soil, then keep them slightly shaded for a few days so plants get off to a good start.

Planting

BURIED TREASURE

Plants like to grow in warm soil, so old-fashioned gardeners with cold, clay soil often buried sheeps' wool in a trench and worked it into the soil before planting. Sheeps' wool helped the clods of clay to break down, improving the aeration and drainage of the soil and therefore helping it to warm quicker. This is like adding sand or grit to soil to lighten it and improve drainage, but sheeps' wool also breaks down to provide nutrients.

Another practice was to bury hair around a plant's roots when planting, or to line a trench with it. This was designed to snare or cut pests trying to crawl over it. Hair also contains some vital minerals and micronutrients not otherwise readily available. Bury banana skins just under the soil to supply roses and herbaceous plants with magnesium, sulfur, calcium, phosphates, silica, and sodium. Old boots were also often buried as slow release fertilizer, but don't try this unless your footwear is made completely of leather.

TIP

• When buying nursery-grown specimens, buy plants in flower so that you can see what you're getting, but remember that container-grown plants will probably flower earlier than they will in your garden the next year.

• Plant after 4:00 p.m. – then the sun's heat is decreasing in intensity and plants have a chance to settle in during the coolest part of the day.

MYTH BUSTER

For centuries, throughout Europe, gardeners were advised to bury a dead sheep or cow under a vine or fig. This is based on sound practice: blood meal and bone meal are two of the best slow-release organic fertilizers, and a rotting carcass attracts biological organisms that keep the soil beautifully crumbly and aerated, so the plant's roots can get at the nutrients in the well-fertilized soil. Take care, however, to keep animal waste out of the kitchen garden to avoid diseases that could be transmitted to people.

VINE

POTTING OUT

Step 1
Dig a hole about twice the width of the container and several inches deeper. Mix the soil you have removed with compost or well-rotted manure.

Step 2
Place one hand firmly around the base of the plant and over the compost. Invert the pot, tap the bottom to loosen the plant, and gently ease out the plant.

Step 3
Gently separate any tangled roots, trimming back thick roots if necessary. But leave fibrous roots intact and with as much compost as possible around them.

Step 4
Place plant in prepared hole with the top of the potting medium at soil level. Lay a cane on the soil to check.

Step 5
Backfill the hole with the prepared soil, firming the soil around the plant with your hand or heel. Water thoroughly.

JUNK POTS

If you want to plant in containers, there are lots of junk options. Broken trash cans or old food cans are good pots for plants as long as you make holes in the bottom for drainage and line the base with a few stones or a handful of gravel. Broken wicker baskets are excellent lightweight containers; just line the inside with moss or plastic bags to keep moisture in. Old barrels make great tubs for potatoes or strawberries, especially in gardens where space is limited.

FOOD CAN CONTAINER

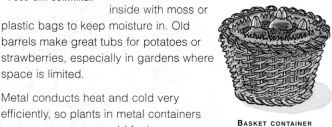

BASKET CONTAINER

Metal conducts heat and cold very efficiently, so plants in metal containers could fry in summer and freeze in winter. After ensuring adequate drainage, line a metal pot with plastic or old bubble wrap to insulate the roots against being baked. When using old cans, remember that the cut edge at the top is sharp and dangerous. Tape the cans around the top before planting.

BARREL POT

57

THE SOWING CALENDAR

BEFORE CALENDARS, PEOPLE KNEW WHEN TO PLANT BY THE SEASONS, THE WEATHER, AND KNOWLEDGE PASSED DOWN THROUGH GENERATIONS. RHYMES, STORIES, AND SAYINGS MADE SOWING TIMES EASY TO REMEMBER.

*Sow your cucumbers in March
You will need neither bag nor sack.
Sow them in April
You will have few.
I will sow mine in May
And I will have more than you.*
Cucumbers need long daylight hours, warmth, and steady moisture, but they don't appreciate cold winds or downpours. Hence the saying, which applies to planting cucumbers outdoors, not in the greenhouse.

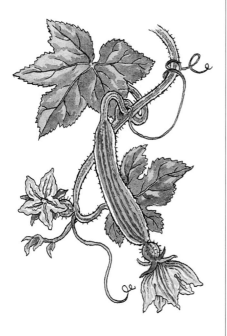

*When elm leaves are as big as a shilling
Plant kidney beans if to plant 'em you're willing.
When elm leaves are as big as a penny
You must plant beans if you mean to have any.*
Elms are among the earliest trees to leaf in spring, and many old sayings remind people to plant when the elm leaves appear.

On St. Valentine's Day sow beans in the clay, or *On Candlemas Day* (Feb. 2) *sow beans in the clay.*
In 1752 the Gregorian calendar replaced the Julian calendar in North America and the United Kingdom, so 11 days were lost and Candlemas Day was followed the day after by St. Valentine's Day.

Plant garden beans when the sign is in the scales; they will hang full refers to moon planting, under the sign of Libra.

Sow peas and beans on St. David's or St. Chad's (Mar. 1 and 2), *be the weather good or bad.*
It became the practice to sow sweet peas on St. Patrick's Day (March 17) for the most fragrant flowers. In North America, potatoes are also planted on this day.

When the oak puts on his gosling gray, 'tis time to sow barley, night and day.

Good Friday was traditionally a hectic planting day, the best day for planting potatoes, runner beans, parsley, and others. Good Friday was seen as the day when the devil was powerless, so sowing and planting was safe. It was particularly important to sow parsley then to try to prevent parsley from having to make its obligatory two journeys to Satan before coming up for the gardener. Stories surrounding parsley arose because parsley is tricky to germinate, and it often took three mandatory plantings – two for the devil and one for the gardener – for any crop of worth to appear.

It was also often recommended to pour boiling water over the ground where the parsley was to be sown to deter Satan; some modern gardeners recommend warming the parsley trench before sowing to aid germination.

Good Friday was also known as "Hangman's Day," so hemp seed was traditionally sown then because it was grown to make rope.

Plant trees at All Hallows (Oct. 21) *and you'll be sure they'll prosper. Plant them after Candlemas* (Feb. 2) *and you'll have to beg them to grow.*

This garden lore reflects the fact that you should plant trees in fall so they have a dormant period for their roots to get acclimatized to the ground before starting to grow in spring. If you plant trees after February, they are likely to be stressed, as their sap will be rising and growth beginning.

Who in January sows oats gets groats, indicates that early oat sowing is best.

Plant shallots on the shortest day and harvest on the longest. This is very dependent on your soil conditions, but this prescription reflects imitative magic which was seen to cause the onions to swell with lengthening days.

TAKING CUTTINGS AND DIVIDING PLANTS ARE
SIMPLE AND SATISFYING METHODS OF ACQUIRING
THE EXACT SAME PLANT THAT YOU ADMIRE IN A
FRIEND'S OR NEIGHBOR'S GARDEN.

LILY

Making more

Gardeners for centuries had very similar plants in their gardens.
But during the 18th and 19th centuries all sorts of exciting
plants began to arrive in the gardens of the wealthy as a result
of increased travel, trade, and exploration. These gradually
spread to neighboring gardens through cuttings and divisions.

WILLOW WATER

Step 1
Cut fresh willow stems
into pieces 1 inch
(25 mm) long. Cut
enough to fill the
bottom of a large
coffee can about 2
inches (50 mm) deep.

Step 2
Add warm, not hot,
water to cover the
stem pieces by an
extra 1 inch (25 mm).

Step 3
Cover the can with
its lid and let the
willow pieces soak for
48 hours.

Step 4
Remove the stem
pieces, then place your
cuttings into the water,
and let them stand in
the water for 24 hours
before planting.

SUCCESSFUL CUTTINGS

All you need for successful cuttings is a healthy
parent plant, and a pot of rooting medium. This
should be low in nutrients, well drained, and
aerated, such as sand mixed with potting soil.
To be sure of success, dip or soak the ends of
your cuttings in a rooting hormone. This is a
commercially available synthetic imitation of
growth hormones, such as gibberellin, naturally
available in plants. Willow water is an alternative
homemade rooting medium (see left).

Take cuttings from strongly growing shoots on
your chosen plant. Cut from spring-flowering
plants in summer, and from summer-flowering
plants in spring before they bud. Simply cut off
a piece of stem about 6 in (15 cm) long. Remove
leaves from the bottom third of the stem, being sure to leave at least two leaves
or pairs of leaves, then place this end into your prepared rooting medium. Insert
cuttings by half their length into the rooting medium. Keep cuttings sprayed with
water until you cover the pot, then water, cover with plastic, and put in a cool place.

In frost-free gardens you can plant cuttings right in a sheltered trench filled with
a mixture of soil, compost, and sand. Dip the ends of your cuttings in rooting
medium before planting them, and make sure the soil stays evenly moist.

⟳ **Dip the stems of cuttings into
hormone rooting medium for
the most reliable propagation.**

MYTH BUSTER

MYTH BUSTER

Cuttings need moisture to help them root, but they will rot with too much humidity. So keep them covered with a plastic bag, but take it off and turn it inside out before replacing it, whenever you notice condensation. Roots should form within three or four weeks. The rooting medium is low in nutrients, so spray the new plants with diluted liquid fertilizer, such as seaweed. Don't disturb the cuttings until fall or spring when you pot them in small individual pots in good all-purpose potting soil.

BEGONIAS

TIP

Always take cuttings or divide plants on a cool day, preferably in damp weather, and water the parent plant first. This causes the least stress.

ROOT CUTTINGS AND LAYERS

Begonias and some other plants will happily root in a glass of water. Mint (*Mentha* spp.) and horseradish *(Armoracia rusticana)* can be increased by taking a section of root and planting it elsewhere in the garden. In fact, both plants are rampant, so you may wish to restrict root growth by planting them in a container.

Most woody herbs will form new roots where a section of stem is pegged into the ground. After rooting, cut the resulting plants from the parent plant and replant.

DIVIDING AND LAYERING

Plants that are a few years old can be increased by division in spring or fall. All you do is divide a plant's root system in two. Some vigorous plants may be quite happy to be sliced with a spade, but it is best to use two forks back-to-back to give maximum leverage and least disturbance to the root system.

Divide established plants by inserting two forks, back-to-back, into the clump and gently prying them apart.

ROSE

MYTH BUSTER

Snowdrops *(Galanthus* spp.*)* should be lifted and divided immediately after flowering. Other bulbs, such as tulips *(Tulipa* spp.*),* are often lifted when their leaves die down, stored in a dry place, then replanted for the following year. Often, if left in the ground, mice will feast on them.

AFRICAN MARIGOLD

BEFORE ANYONE HAD HEARD OF PLANT SYMBIOSIS, GARDENERS KNEW WHICH PLANTS HELPED THEIR NEIGHBORS, AND WHICH SEEMED TO HAVE THE OPPOSITE EFFECT. YOU CAN STILL USE THIS KNOWLEDGE TODAY FOR A HEALTHY GARDEN.

Plant partnerships

Plants can be good companions for many reasons. One may shelter or support another, provide extra nutrients to benefit a neighbor, repel pests from other plants, or keep diseases away. This can be due to size and habit, to scent, or to oils, hormones, and enzymes given off through roots and leaves.

GOOD NEIGHBORS

One of the best-known good neighbor plants is the African marigold (*Tagetes erecta*). From the 16th century on, gardeners welcomed it into their gardens for its color, shape, and foliage. Soon they discovered that other plants seemed to flourish when marigolds were planted nearby. We now know that the strongly scented foliage and flowers repel flying pests from nearby plants, and secretions from their roots inhibit weeds and kill parasitic worms called nematodes, which destroy vegetable crops.

PEAS

Peas and beans are excellent companions for other species because their roots fix nitrogen in the soil for other plants to enjoy. Before threshers, farmers often grew cereals mixed with beans and peas; this made the crops flourish as well as providing increased nutrition for the cattle.

Another old favorite is the foxglove (*Digitalis* spp.). These were once among the most common flowers in many gardens, grown not just for their beauty, but because they stimulate growth of other plants and help disease resistance. Moreoever, if you grow them in the orchard or vegetable garden, they improve the storage qualities of fruit and vegetables. This is probably largely because of beneficial gaseous secretions as well as minute amounts of hormones given off by foxgloves. Root vegetables store better if grown near foxgloves.

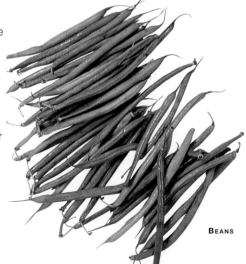

BEANS

MYTH BUSTER

Marigolds are not good for everything! Don't plant them in the herbaceous border, except right at the edge, because their root secretions can also inhibit the growth of some herbaceous plants.

APPLE TREE

STRAWBERRY

Plants that make good neighbors

Apples, wallflowers, chives, nasturtiums
Asparagus, tomatoes
Beans, marigolds, squash, corn
Carrots, beans, onions, garlic, chives, tomatoes
Beets, onions, lettuce, cabbage
Borage, tomatoes, strawberries
Potatoes, beans, brassicas, peas, corn
Grapes, hyssop, lavender
Sunflowers, squash, corn, cucumbers
Tomatoes, parsley, basil, carrots, asparagus, onions
Lettuce, carrots, squash, radishes
Peas, garlic
Turnips, peas

CABBAGE

ASPARAGUS

Plants that are not good neighbors

Rue and basil
Runner beans and potatoes
Beets and beans
Beans and onions and garlic
Strawberries and cabbage
Gladioli and beans
Tomatoes and gooseberries

TOMATOES

GOOD FRIENDS

Wallflowers *(Erysimum cheiri)* were planted in orchards for centuries. They flower early in the year, so they encourage insects, which are then attracted to fruit blossoms to ensure pollination. Nasturtiums *(Tropaeolum majus)* lure aphids from apple trees and attract blackfly away from vegetables.

Onions and garlic, as well as others in the Allium family, make powerful friends. All seem to have some success as fungicides and insecticides, perhaps because they accumulate sulfur very efficiently, and many pests avoid its odor.

Among the many herbs that benefit vegetables with their strong scent (see page136), Chamomile *(Anthemis nobilis/Matricaria chamomilla)* has long been valued in the vegetable plot. As well as the "sweet breath" of its leaf exudations described by 17th century writers, it brings potassium, sulfur, and calcium to the surface of the soil, making these nutrients available to roots of companion plants, and it hosts helpful hoverflies and wasps.

MYTH BUSTER

One plant to site carefully is the strongly scented rue. Long connected with magic and curses, many old-fashioned gardeners won't grow it all. Some plant lore suggests that rue *(Ruta graveolens)* will make sage *(Salvia officinalis)* poisonous if planted next to it, but there seems no reason to believe this. However, its root secretions damage brassicas, and may prevent basil from growing. Its leaf exudations prevent seeds from germinating. Some people are allergic to the oils in its leaves.

Moon

MANY GARDENERS BELIEVE THAT
VEGETABLES SHOULD BE PLANTED
DURING SPECIFIC PHASES OF THE
MOON FOR BEST GROWTH AND FLAVOR,
OR ON DATES MADE FAVORABLE BY THE
MOVEMENT OF THE OTHER PLANETS.

The moon influences all the water on Earth, from the tides of the oceans to the movement of water in plants' cells.

MYTH BUSTER

Belief in moon gardening occurs in many cultures. New Zealand Maoris believe that the moon protects crops, and they only plant sweet potatoes on the 11th, 27th, and 28th days of the lunar month, using long spades with crescents carved into the handles. An old English saying "light Christmas, light harvest" means that if there is a full moon at Christmas, the next harvest will be poor.

It has been widely believed through the ages that sowing and planting when the moon is waxing ensures rapid germination and growth. Another idea is that vegetables that grow underground or need to develop slowly should be planted in the dark of the moon, when it is waning, and those that grow above ground should be planted in the waxing or full moon. This may sound like superstition, but that doesn't mean that it won't work. Even gardeners who otherwise have little time for moon gardening often follow the advice to "Plant potatoes when the moon is on the wane, they want to grow down that is plain."

POTATOES

Plant crops that produce seeds on the inside, like melons and peppers, between the first quarter of the waxing moon and the full moon.

FACT OR FANTASY

Some people say that moon gardening works because all water is affected by the movement of the moon, and plants are largely water. Both the sun and moon affect water through their magnetic pull, but the moon is much closer to earth, so its influence is greater. In addition to the simple notion of planting crops that go upward in the increasing moon and plants that go down when it is decreasing, different plants' water requirements are different. When water is rising during the waxing moon, seeds sown and crops planted can more easily take up water than those sown in the waning or decreasing phase. So crops that thrive in dry conditions are planted during the waning phase, and crops that need lots of water, during the waxing phase.

MYTH BUSTER

Lunar cycles can influence the activity, behavior, and breeding of animals. Plants are most vulnerable to predators in the first few days after germination, so planting at a phase of the moon when pests are active could reduce the yield. For example, many small rodents forage for food most at new moon when they are least at risk from owls, so this is a bad time for planting corn.

EXPOSURE TO LIGHT

The main environmental factor triggering flowering is exposure to light or photoperiodism, especially the length of the night. Plants can respond to light levels much lower than those experienced at full moon, so it would be surprising if they did not respond to the phases of the moon. If we assume that moonlight can affect the flowering times of plants, then the distinction between sowing some plants in the lighter phases and some in the darker phases of the moon makes sense. Flowering is usually undesirable in most "below ground" crops; but is necessary for many of the "above ground" crops, such as sweet corn, peas, and beans.

Plant crops that have seeds on the outside, like asparagus and cabbage, in the first week after the new moon.

Moon gardeners also look to the signs of the zodiac and the qualities of each sign and planet to influence planting and harvesting.

CAPRICORN
(Feminine) Earthy and productive (Semifruitful)

AQUARIUS
(Masculine) Barren and dry

PISCES
(Feminine) Fruitful and watery

ARIES
(Masculine) Barren, dry, and fiery

TAURUS
(Feminine) Productive, moist, and earthy (Semifruitful)

GEMINI
(Masculine) Barren, dry, and airy

CANCER
(Feminine) Fruitful, moist, and watery

LEO
(Masculine) Barren, dry, and fiery

VIRGO
(Feminine) Barren, moist, and earthy

LIBRA
(Masculine) Fruitful, moist, and airy

SCORPIO
(Feminine) Fruitful, moist, and watery

SAGITTARIUS
(Masculine) Barren, dry, and fiery

CHAPTER 4

CARING FOR PLANTS

YOU DON'T NEED LOTS OF TIME OR MONEY TO GROW A BEAUTIFUL AND PRODUCTIVE GARDEN. BUT YOU DO NEED TO GIVE YOUR PLANTS WHAT THEY NEED TO FLOURISH: A BALANCED DIET, THE RIGHT AMOUNT OF WATER, AND PROTECTION FROM THE ELEMENTS.

AFTER YOU'VE BEEN GARDENING FOR A FEW YEARS, YOU WILL PROBABLY BE ABLE TO RECOGNIZE WHAT YOUR PLANTS NEED JUST BY LOOKING AT THEM. UNTIL THEN, THE BEST WAY TO LEARN IS TO FOLLOW PRACTICES THAT HAVE BEEN PROVEN TO WORK FOR CENTURIES, AND AMEND THEM TO SUIT YOUR GARDEN AND LIFESTYLE IF NECESSARY.

THE BEST WAY TO FEED PLANTS IS TO GIVE THEM WELL-NURTURED SOIL, BUT SOMETIMES YOU NEED TO FEED PLANTS WITHOUT DIGGING THE SOIL. USE MULCHES AND LIQUID FERTILIZERS INSTEAD.

Mulches & teas

Partially rotted straw makes an excellent mulch for herbaceous beds, but rake it off in fall and replace with compost, manure, or rotted leaves.

Squash and pumpkins are greedy feeders and benefit from mulches of manure or drinks of manure tea.

MULCH

Mulch is a layer of material spread on a bed or border, or around individual plants. Sometimes you want to feed your plants without digging, and mulches can provide lasting, slow-release fertilizer. They also help to conserve water and suppress weeds.

Manure is an old favorite mulch, and it is ideal for roses and perennials. But it should be well composted before it is applied to the garden. Autumn leaves are free and slowly provide nutrients and organic matter to soil, but it is better to wait to use them until they have been composted for a year. Wood chips are attractive and long lasting, but don't use fresh ones, which will tie up soil nitrogen as they decompose. Use composted chips instead. Spent mushroom compost is also an excellent mulch.

MULCHING ONIONS

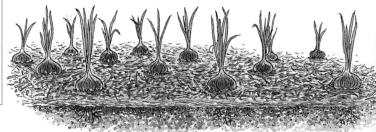

MYTH BUSTER

Fresh lawn clippings make an excellent weed-suppressing and nutritious mulch around onions and most vegetables. Spread a thin layer and add to it over several weeks, or the mulch may heat up excessively. Never use clippings from a lawn that has been dosed with chemicals because these can inhibit other plants' growth patterns. Compost treated lawn clippings in a pile on their own to heat up and destroy any chemical residues before using.

LIQUID GOLD

Every garden has room for a pile of compost or manure. As well as being excellent soil conditioners they can be made into liquid fertilizers. Fill a bucket half-way with compost or manure, and then fill it to the rim with water. Leave it for a day, then strain it and dilute the liquid until it is a warm amber color. Pour it from a watering can around ornamental plants in spring for a quick nutrient boost, or for pick-me-up feedings during the year. Use weak manure tea instead of water for heavy-feeding plants such as brassicas and squashes. But keep it away from herbs, and don't splash it on plant leaves or vegetables before harvesting.

Comfrey tea *(Symphytum* spp.*)* is one of the best fertilizers, but it can be rather smelly when it's brewing! Steep armfuls of comfrey leaves in a covered tank of water for a few weeks; then use the liquid all around your garden at any time of year to supply minerals and aid general health. Comfrey tea also boosts tired houseplants. Horsetail tea *(Equisetum arvense)* is another mineral-rich additive, but horsetails are slower to rot.

MYTH BUSTER

Wood-ash tea is recommended in some old manuals as the best high-potassium amendment for tomatoes. But ash can create salt imbalances in the soil, so it is best not used. Check commercial fish products – many have decent amounts of postassium and can be made into liquid feeds.

TIP

• Always mulch in damp weather, or water your beds well first. Your ground should stay moist under the layer of covering. If you mulch in dry weather, water will have a hard time getting through to the soil and the roots of your plants.

• To lessen the smell of comfrey tea, let comfrey leaves compost in an old tank or tub without adding water. They rot down into a thick liquid, which you can then dilute with water as you use it.

○ If you find that steeping comfrey tea in water is too smelly, let comfrey leaves compost in a tub, tank – or even a bucket – without adding water. This will eventually rot down into a thick liquid, which you can dilute with water as you use it.

Compost
Most valuable used on vegetable crops with a long growing period.

Well-rotted manure
Perfect around heavy feeders such as blackcurrants. Reduces black-spot on roses.

Straw
Use partially rotted straw around perennials, but don't incorporate it into the soil or it may rob nitrogen. Use under strawberries and squash to keep fruit clean.

Hay
Excellent nutrient provider and insulation for cold soils. Good around fruit trees and bushes.

Mushroom compost
Never use on acid-loving plants, such as rhododendrons or azaleas.

Wood chips/shredded bark
Use on established plants, not seedlings.

Autumn leaves
Use well-rotted, otherwise they can be acid. Makes an attractive mulch for flower borders.

SOME PLANTS WILL
GROW BETTER WITH
LITTLE OR NO EXTRA
ATTENTION, WHEREAS
OTHERS NEED A
HELPING HAND.
LEARN TO RECOGNIZE
THE SIGNS AND YOU
CAN HELP YOUR
PLANTS THRIVE.

When to feed

⭕ As a general rule, feed the soil,
not the plant. You should only
need to give plants extra
nourishment while you are
building up your healthy soil.

MYTH BUSTER

Extra feeding does not make extra-strong
plants. Plants fed with high-nitrogen fertilizers
produce masses of foliage at the expense of
fruits and flowers, because the plants put
their energy into growing bigger quicker.
They perform poorly and the succulent
growth is vulnerable to pests and diseases.

GERANIUMS

LISTENING TO YOUR PLANTS

There are plenty of common signs when a plant is stressed, but
this doesn't mean that they need more food. A wilting plant is
more likely to need water than food; limp or curling leaves may
indicate pests or diseases; and a plant producing leaves but no
flowers may be over-nourished rather than under-nourished.

A balanced soil provides all that a plant needs. So follow the
old adage "Feed the soil, not the plant." As a rule, feed plants
less, not more. Seedlings should need no more than occasional
watering with dilute liquid fertilizer, and mature plants can only
absorb extra nutrients when growing vigorously before fruiting
and flowering. Never feed once fruits or flowers have formed
because the plants' energies are all going into production of the
next generation, and they won't welcome the distraction of extra
root or leaf stimulation. Never feed dormant plants.

Milk is good for plants. Gardeners used to rinse out milk churns
onto the garden, and found plants fed with the vitamin- and
mineral-rich milky water thrived. Tea is also a boost for acid-
loving camellias (Camellia spp.) and geraniums (Pelargonium
spp.), and the tannic acid helps keep pests and diseases away.

A BALANCED DIET

The most important elements in the soil that plants need are nitrogen (N), potassium (K), and phosporus (P). Nitrogen promotes vigorous leaf and stem growth, phosphorus assists strong root growth, and potassium stimulates flowering and fruiting. If plants are rather stunted or spindly with pale leaves, perhaps with a yellowish or pink tinge, they might need a nitrogen boost. This happens most often in poor soils, or in containers. The best solution is to sprinkle a little high-nitrogen fertilizer, such as bloodmeal or soybean meal, around your plant, or plant green manures in the soil the following season.

If the leaves of fruit trees and bushes look slightly scorched with brown blotches on the edges, and fruits don't form well, try adding a high-potassium fertilizer such as greensand. Plants grown in soils with the wrong pH find it difficult to get at adequate potassium in the soil. Phosphorus deficiency is rarer and more difficult to see, but if plant growth is persistently slow and young foliage is dull and yellowish, you may need to provide extra bonemeal or phosphate rock.

In very wet summers, magnesium and iron may be leached out of the soil, causing leaves to yellow between the veins, and leaves may fall early. A simple traditional magnesium boost is to water the roots or leaves with Epsom salts diluted 8 oz in 18 pints (220 g in 10 L) of water.

SPECIAL CASES

Windowboxes, hanging baskets, and containers have special feeding requirements; as the plants' roots are restricted, and they are not planted in a living, balanced soil. Feed regularly with liquid seaweed or compost tea (see page 69), and if you are growing perennials in pots, topdress every winter and spring with compost. Do not use phosphorus-rich fertilizers, because these promote vigorous root growth.

Plants in containers cannot get everything they need from the soil, so feed them regularly with liquid fertilizer, but avoid comfrey tea as it promotes too vigorous growth.

PLANTS ARE ABOUT 90 PERCENT WATER,
SO THE CRITICAL ROLE OF WATER IN OUR
GARDENS COMES AS NO SURPRISE.

Watering

TIP

Don't over-water plants in heavy soils that don't drain well. Red hot pokers (*Kniphofia* spp.*)* and penstemons (*Penstemon* spp.*)* are among the plants that hate water-logged roots; alpine plants and strawberries die; bulbs and corms rot.

When and how much to water can be big questions for inexperienced gardeners. Plants growing in full sun obviously use and lose more water than those growing in shady conditions, but other factors are also important. Some plants grow faster than others, which affects the amount of water they use, and when plants are small, their roots are nearer the surface so they will lose more moisture than deep-rooted plants through surface evaporation.

SLOW WATERING

"Water seedlings at the end of the day, their roots must go down it is plain to say." Plant roots need to be able to delve as deeply as possible into the soil to get their water and nutrients rather than stay near the surface. Slow, deep soakings are much more beneficial than surface watering or quick floods where half the water runs away. This promotes deep root growth and makes plants more tolerant of dry spells.

YOUNG SEEDLINGS

MYTH BUSTER

Although water is critical, we can give our plants too much. Most plants in temperate regions need about an inch of water per week (see page 74 for tips on collecting water). If you give them too much, their ability to absorb and use the water will be impaired because plants need to be able to draw oxygen from the soil along with the water and nutrients. Oxygen is not accessible in very wet soil.

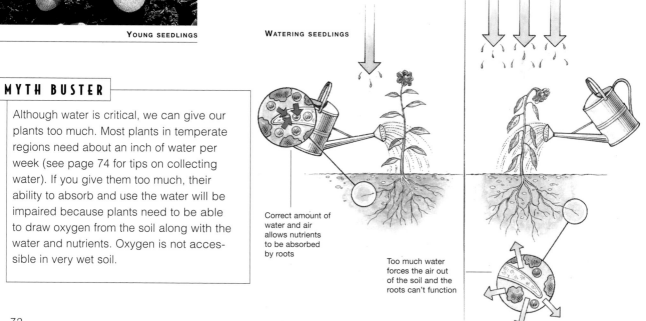

WATERING SEEDLINGS

Correct amount of water and air allows nutrients to be absorbed by roots

Too much water forces the air out of the soil and the roots can't function

CONTAINERS AND HANGING BASKETS

Plants grown in containers always need more moisture than those growing in the soil because their roots are restricted, there is a high proportion of root to soil, and containers dry out fast. Use moisture-retaining granules or gel in the soil mix for ornamentals and soak baskets twice a day in high summer.

For slow-release watering in a hanging basket or container, place six to ten ice cubes on the soil, hidden under foliage.

WATER EARLY IN THE DAY

On hot days some of your plants may begin to wilt, but never water them in full sunshine. Up to half of the water will be lost through evaporation, and any that falls on the leaves will catch the sun's rays, heat up, and scorch the plant. The best time to water is early in the day, before the sun is overhead. If you water at the coolest times of day, the plant is in a receptive state to absorb and use it readily. But never water plants in the evening when you suspect frost: if excess water is not absorbed into the soil, it can turn to ice and damage the plants.

MYTH BUSTER

Old gardening manuals are full of drawings for watering systems, but in most cases a watering can is all you need. Never use a hose without a watering wand because the pressure turns the surface of the soil to mud, which then bakes hard and makes life harder for the plant.

TIP

Until you get to know your garden, test the soil several times a day to see if your plants need water. It should be moist at the depth of about half an index finger below ground level. If it is dry, water gently at the rate of about 2 pints (1 L) per square yard (meter). Repeat every few hours if necessary. You will soon get a feel for how much water your plants need, and before long you'll know when to water just by looking at them.

WATERING CAN

Test the soil with your finger. If it is dry at half a finger's depth, you should water gently.

73

What kind of water

RAINWATER IS USUALLY RECOMMENDED AS THE HEALTHIEST DRINK FOR YOUR PLANTS, BUT YOU CAN ALSO USE TAP WATER OR FOLLOW TRADITIONAL RECYCLING PRACTICES.

In the days before running water, gardeners would not waste freshly drawn water on the garden. They caught rainwater in water barrels and tubs and used this, and water that had been used for cooking, washing, or cleaning was sloshed onto the garden. These are both excellent practices today, but be careful how you store and use the water.

MAGIC WATER

Some biodynamic gardeners follow an ancient practice of enlivening the water for their gardens. They take a tub of rainwater and stir it with a wooden spoon or paddle clockwise for 40 turns, then reverse the direction to turn it counterclockwise 40 times. Some of this water is then poured into a spiral-shaped cow's horn and buried in the ground for a year to mature. This is justified by modern science: water that goes through a spiraling shape picks up energy. Water that is full of energy will interact better with all it comes into contact with, and promote better growth in plants.

Use rainwater in orchards and graywater on shrubs – never use graywater on food plants.

MYTH BUSTER

Gardening books used to recommend that the best refreshment for your plants was rainwater that had been stored for several weeks. Rainwater is certainly better for plants than tapwater in hardwater areas with high calcium deposits, but stagnant water is dangerous. You must cover your storage container. Exposure to light affects water and turns it stagnant quickly in hot, dry weather. The water then contains numerous micro-organisms and bacteria that spread diseases, and may hinder the roots taking up the nutrients they need.

Always cover a water barrel to keep water fresh longer, and so that insects cannot lay their eggs there.

TIP

If you have no rainwater, run tap water into a watering can and allow it to settle for an hour before using it on precious seedlings. This allows any chlorine in the water to evaporate before you use it on young plants.

RHODODENDRON

RECYCLED WATER

Dishwater and bathwater, known collectively as graywater, can be used on most trees, shrubs, and nonedible plants unless your household water is treated with water softeners. However, you must only use graywater containing bio-degradeable household detergents and soaps; never use graywater that contains any chem-icals or bleach; these will affect the soil and the ability of plants to take up nutrients – and may contaminate the water table.

WATER STORAGE

To avoid any possibility of a buildup of bacteria in your soil, it is wise to alternate graywater use with fresh water. It may be a good idea to run the water from your sink through a sieve to avoid spreading old food particles on the garden, although natural fats in graywater will do no harm to plants, and roses thrive on them. Collect the waste water in a holding tank with a lid – a plastic trash can is ideal – but use graywater within 48 hours. Do not store it for longer, because it gets very smelly and attracts insects and undesirable bacteria. Note: some municipalities prohibit the use of graywater, so be sure to check local ordinances before watering plants with graywater.

WITH TRENDS TOWARD HIGHER SUMMER
TEMPERATURES AND LOWER LEVELS OF WINTER
RAINFALL, ALL GARDENERS SHOULD BECOME
INCREASINGLY AWARE OF THE NEED TO WATER
EFFICIENTLY AND CONSERVE WHAT THEY CAN.

Saving water

> **TIP**
>
> Soaker hoses work best in short lengths, and in gardens sloping away from the water source. If you need to water an upward-sloping bed, you need to place your water source as near to the bed as possible.

Traditional gardeners did not have running water, so water was a precious resource. They knew how to look after their soil and to plant crops that matured at different times so soil was usually covered to prevent water evaporation. Even though we have running water now, when the water supply is limited, as in very hot summers, or if you are going to be away from your garden for some time, you need to look at different options.

HOME-MADE HOSE

Garden stores sell all sorts of water-conserving devices, but you can make your own. Soaker or seep hoses are a good option, particularly in beds of vegetables or perennials. Pierce a length of hose with tiny pinprick holes along its length and lay it among your plants, attaching one end to the faucet or another low-pressure water supply.

> **MYTH BUSTER**
>
> Squash are known today as very thirsty feeders in the garden, but old-fashioned gardeners never watered them. They grew squash directly on the compost heap, where the squash drew all the moisture and nutrients they needed.

SQUASH

Mulch fruit trees well in spring with half-rotted straw, compost, or strawy manure.

REACHING THE ROOTS

Trees need plenty of water to get going and form healthy root systems. To make sure water goes just where it's needed, after planting a new tree, drive four sections of 2-ft (60-cm) long plastic pipe 2-4 in (5-10 cm) in diameter into the ground around the tree about 1 yd (1 m) from the tree trunk. Leave about 4 in (10 cm) above ground level and water directly into these pipes every week in dry weather, filling them to the top. The water will slowly seep down to where the tree needs it most. You can remove the pipes after two summers.

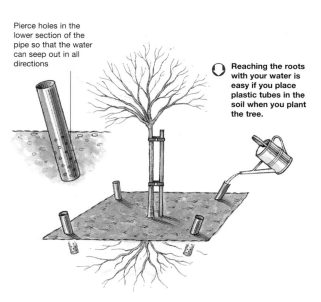

Pierce holes in the lower section of the pipe so that the water can seep out in all directions

Reaching the roots with your water is easy if you place plastic tubes in the soil when you plant the tree.

WHEN YOU'RE NOT AT HOME

If you can't find a neighbor to come and tend your plants when you go away, precious specimens can be helped by watering them, then mulching well, and covering much of the plants with straw to insulate them. Move container-grown plants into the shade and stand them in buckets or trays of shallow water.

Clear plastic 4 pint (2 L) soda bottles make good emergency watering systems. Turn them upside down in your beds or pots and fill them with water for slow-release watering. Another favorite method is to seal the drainage holes in some terracotta pots and sink them into your beds. Keep them filled with water. The pots are porous, and when they are in contact with soil the water is drawn out of the pot through surface tension and osmosis. If you use terracotta plant saucers, they'll serve double-duty as bird baths.

TIP

Plant groundcover plants as living mulch to conserve moisture in the soil.

MATCH YOUR PLANTS

Traditional country gardens in a particular region always boasted a similar array of plants. This was not lack of imagination, but because people had learned by experimentation what would grow most easily in the areas. They might lavish attention on one or two special plants to show their skill, but in general they grew what suited the soil. Match plants to the conditions you can give them, and try not to be tempted to plant moisture-lovers in hot, dry spots. If you have an arid garden, choose Mediterranean or plantings native to your region rather than herbaceous plants; you will be able to get as much variety, and gardening will be much more pleasurable than if you are constantly struggling against nature.

A living layer of plants keeps moisture from evaporating from the soil.

PLANTS SOMETIMES NEED SUPPORT TO STAND UP TO DRYING WINDS, FIERCE SUN, OR FREEZING WEATHER. PLAN YOUR GARDEN SO THAT NEIGHBORING PLANTS CAN OFFER OTHERS PROTECTION, AND FOLLOW THESE TRADITIONAL GARDENING METHODS.

Plant protection

If you want salad greens to grow in a hot garden, grow heat-seeking corn to give shade to the salad plants, or plant sunflowers to block sun from brassicas and cucumbers. Stake the sunflowers and allow cucumbers to climb up their stems. Plant spring-flowering bulbs under trees, where soil won't be too wet.

In dry, windy gardens, plant seeds or seedlings in trenches so that water runs off the soil straight to the plants, and seedlings are protected from wind. Or plant hedges or barriers, such as woven willow fences for windbreaks.

Decorative woven willow or hazel plant surrounds protect plants from wind and lend them support.

MYTH BUSTER

Squash, corn, and beans have been cultivated in the Americas since ancient times, and are often referred to as the "three sisters." Although the term came to have some magical associations, it was based on fact. The three crops benefitted each other as they grew. The beans fixed nitrogen in the soil for growth; the corn stalks provided supports for the beans to climb; and the spreading vines and large leaves of squashes kept the soil cool and moist. The crops also provided a diet balanced in carbohydrates and vegetable protein.

WINTER PROTECTION

Tender plants need to be moved inside for the winter in frost-prone areas. Frost will scorch and kill leaves of evergreen plants and rot stems of some perennials when they freeze and thaw. Semi-hardy specimens, such as French lavender (*Lavandula stoechas*) and Myrtle (*Myrtus communis*) can live outside if you protect them, depending how cold the winters are in your region. Cover them in straw and wrap them in burlap, tied tight enough to keep it from blowing away. Or mound 4 inch (10 cm) thick heaps of straw around them.

FRENCH LAVENDER

FOAM PEANUTS

ALTERNATIVE PROTECTION

Old packing materials are a boon to thrifty gardeners. Use bubble wrap to protect delicate specimens, such as topiarized bay trees (*Laurus nobilis*) – see page 80 – or fig trees in winter, or to line the windows of a greenhouse or conservatory.

Don't try to clear snow away from plants. It provides a good insulating layer. But shake the branches of trees to dislodge snow, as the weight can crack and break tree limbs.

PROTECTIVE CURTAIN

Step 1
In late fall, attach 1 in (25 mm) diameter poles to exposed walls above espaliered trees and climbers. Hang a curtain of row-cover fabric from each pole, attaching the fabric with loops of twine.

Step 2
In the evenings, draw this curtain in front of the plants by hooking a bamboo cane through the end curtain loop. This protects your plants from frost.

Plastic soda bottles protect young seedlings – but remove them on very hot days.

SEEDLING HELP

Keep newly planted seedlings shaded for a few days for increased survival and better growth. Large leaves, such as rhubarb or bracken, provide shade but can encourage slugs, so use boxes, cartons, or flowerpots. Or follow an old country custom and lay hedgerow branches across trenches for ten days or so. Protect seedlings from pests; cover plants with sleeves made from cut-off plastic bottles or wiremesh.

MOST PLANTS NEED
TO BE PRUNED
OCCASIONALLY TO
STAY STRONG AND
HEALTHY. MOWING
GRASS IS JUST A
TYPE OF PRUNING.

Pruning

The most important rule in pruning
is always to make a clean cut with
sharp pruners.

> **TIP**
>
> "See through a rose, but
> keep box tight" reminds
> pruners to aim to leave the
> center of a rose bush open
> so that air can circulate and
> discourage fungal infections
> like black spot. However,
> prune evergreens in a solid
> shape. Old advice also
> recommends pruning roses
> in a waxing moon in Oct-
> ober, so they have the
> chance to gather strength
> before winter sets in.

PRUNING MAINTAINS STRENGTH

A fruit tree that is unpruned will become less productive;
unpruned roses will get woody with few blossoms; unpruned
bushes and trees can be more susceptible to pests and
diseases. Unfortunately many people see pruning as a mystery,
not helped by strange advice given through the centuries. A
popular 17th century book said "You are to prune both tops and
roots of every tree you plant," but pruning is just about cutting
out old growth to allow new shoots to come through.

Most summer-flowering trees and shrubs should be pruned in
winter when they are dormant. But those that flower earlier
should be pruned after they flower. An old rhyme advises when
to prune fruit trees: "When leaves are fallen frosts are nigh, cut
pear and apple wood on high. When leaves have swelled and
frosts are gone, take plums before the fruits hang on."

Topiary is simply stylized pruning. Bird, animal, and
geometric shapes can be achieved without difficulty in
box, yew, or other small-leaved evergreen plants.

> **MYTH BUSTER**
>
> Early gardeners recognized that trees fruited
> better if they were pruned, but thought the
> plants would be "offended," so they "half-
> pruned" lightly, just enough "to cherish the
> sap." Light or half-pruning was also prac-
> ticed to leave "half for the birds."

HEDGE SHEARS

○ Purchase cordon or espalier
fruit trees for growing as
fences or against walls.
Prune unwanted shoots
annually when trees are
dormant, except plums,
which must be pruned
after flowering.

ESPALIER

CORDON

BASIL

KEEPING PLANTS TRIM

"Fine basil desireth it may be her lot to grow as
the gelliflower trim in a pot.

That ladies and gentles to whom ye do serve
may help her as needeth, life to preserve."

Many plants thrive on regular trimming to keep
them from getting straggly. Keep all herbs
trimmed in summer to make them last longer
before flowering and going to seed.

To prevent leafy green vegetables from bolting
in prolonged warm weather, you can root
prune them slightly. Chop around the plants
with a spade about 10 in (24 cm) from the
stems. This will retard their growth so they
are slower to set seed.

PRUNING SHEARS

TIP

Persuade a friend to let you
prune their willow, alder, or
hazel tree. Stick the prunings into a trench prepared
with a mix of soil and compost; water well, and the
sticks will grow. Either prune
them back hard every year
to encourage bushiness, or
weave them together to
make a living latticework.

GRASS MAINTENANCE

The earliest recorded "lawns" were flowery meadows, probably within orchards,
where medieval knights and ladies enjoyed themselves. Long before mowers,
these were simply ripped up and returfed when they got too shabby.

"Set mowers a mowing where meadow is grown, the longer it's standing the
worse to be mown" is advice for the month of June in a 19th century gardener's
almanac. To avoid spending excess time behind a mower, try mowing your grass
during a waning moon. According to old lore it will then grow abnormally slowly,
while if you cut it under the waxing moon it will grow very fast.

TRADITIONAL GARDENERS KNEW HOW TO GET THE MOST OUT OF THEIR GARDENS, WHETHER FOR SHOW OR NOT, ALTHOUGH SOME OLD-FASHIONED THEORIES SEEM UNLIKELY TO BRING REWARDS.

Extraordinary measures

MYTH BUSTER

Whipping trees to make them fruit was an ancient custom. Sometimes the bark of a tree is very tight, with little room for nutrition to flow freely through the cambium layer. If the bark is softened or split in some way, the bark has to grow around that split, making more and looser bark, carrying more nutrients through the tree. In some areas apple trees were threatened with "I'll cut your throat" if they didn't fruit. If the bark was slit with a knife, the tree would often prosper.

TIP

The color of hydrangea flowers *(Hydrangea* spp.*)* does depend on the soil they are grown in. Turn pink hydrangeas blue by burying a handful of rusty nails in the soil.

LUPINES

TRAVELER'S TIPS

From the 17th century onward, flowers were introduced to new habitats by explorers. Suddenly flowers in different shapes and colors were available, and theories grew up about how to change the color and form of existing ones. It was believed that cowslips *(Primula veris)* planted upside down would turn into primroses, and if you fed them bullocks' blood they would turn from yellow to red. Red roses *(Rosa* spp.*)* were grown next to apple trees to turn apples red. To change single flowers into doubles, gardeners were advised to dig them up and walk around a field with them or take them for a ride in a wheelbarrow before replanting them. Pinks *(Dianthus* spp.*)* were a special case: those sown on Good Friday were expected to come up double.

STRAIGHT SPECIMENS

For perfectly straight cucumbers, cut clear plastic tubing into several cucumber-length pieces. Drill two holes in one end on either side of the tube, thread twine through the holes, and hang the tubes beneath each forming cucumber. They should grow into the tubes and stay straight.

You need stone-free light soil for perfectly straight carrots. Make large holes in a seed bed with a broomhandle, and fill them with a mixture of soil, peat, sharp sand, and bone meal, rammed moderately firmly into the holes. Sow two or three seeds in each hole, and when seedlings are growing strongly weed out two. Or fill old half-barrels with sifted sand, soil and bonemeal and sow carrots or parsnips.

STRAIGHT CUCUMBER

AFRICAN DAISIES

SECOND SHOWING

Many herbaceous perennials including lupines *(Lupinus* spp.*)* and delphiniums *(Delphinium* spp.*)* can be encouraged to flower twice in one summer. As soon as they have flowered, cut the flower stalks back to within 6 in (15 cm) of the ground, before the plant has a chance to set seed. It will then try again.

Regular deadheading is another way of ensuring that you have blooms over the longest period, particularly of bedding plants, roses, marigolds *(Tagetes* spp.*)*, cornflowers *(Cyanus* spp.*)*, and most daisy-type flowers.

TIP

• To boost a crop of beans, remove every leaf when they begin to turn limp and fall; then feed with compost tea (see page 69).

• To make sure your red tomatoes color well, prune away a few of the leaves surrounding ripening fruit.

• Tea roses seem to smell stronger if you water them with very diluted tea.

MYTH BUSTER

Gardeners used to feed cabbages with beer for extra growth. Fermented hops were supposed to have the same effect as extremely active compost. Do not use modern beers or lagers, because the chemicals used in the brewing process will hinder rather than help a plant. Feed pumpkins with diluted milk to make them large and fleshy – most plants benefit from protein-rich milk as fertilizer.

If your soil is stony and you want straight carrots or parsnips, grow some in a half barrel or large tub in a gritty soil and sand mix.

HARVEST TIME IS TRADITIONALLY A TIME OF CELEBRATION, REJOICING IN THE REWARDS OF YOUR LABORS IN THE GARDEN. TRIED-AND-TESTED TECHNIQUES CAN HELP YOU MAKE THE MOST OF YOUR PRODUCE.

MYTH BUSTER

Countryfolk used to line slatted boxes with nettle or walnut leaves to store fruit and vegetables. The oils that nettles and walnuts excrete from their leaves seemed to delay the process of decay. Similarly, vegetables grown beside foxgloves *(Digitalis spp.)* have improved storage qualities.

DRYING FRAMES

Step 1
Make two squares from 18 in (45 cm) pieces of timber.

Step 2
Sandwich a piece of fine wire mesh, double thickness muslin, or cheesecloth between the squares.

Step 3
Lay another layer of cloth, or brown paper, over the frames to prevent possible bruising to fruit.

TIP

Store fruit on wooden frames covered in cheesecloth, muslin, or wire mesh. Lay sheets of paper on mesh to prevent damage.

Harvesting

GARLIC

FRUIT

The fruit harvest is eagerly anticipated, but how can you tell when hard fruits are ripe? "When wasps are abroad 'tis time to harvest plums" is sound advice. Wasps are attracted to the sugar in ripe plums. Check if apples and pears are ready by putting your hand under the fruit and lifting it slightly, giving it a gentle twist. If it is ripe, the fruit will easily detach from the tree.

Harvest your peaches and apricots when the skins are covered with fuzzy bloom, and wear cotton gloves to avoid bruising the fruit. Harvest figs when a "tear of juice forms" in the fig's "eye" at the stalk.

MYTH BUSTER

It is widely written that you should not pick blackberries after Michaelmas Day (September 29) or October 10 in older sayings before the Gregorian calendar change of 1752, "because the Devil spits on them." When Satan fell out of heaven he was supposed to have fallen into a blackberry bush, leading to the association. Whatever the reason, it is wise to leave blackberries on the bushes after the beginning of October – they'll be past their prime and good for birds.

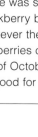

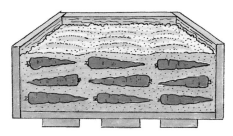

STORING FRUIT

Only sound, unblemished fruit can be stored successfully. Pick apples and pears just before they are ripe by twisting them off the tree and laying them individually into boxes. After a couple of weeks wrap each one in tissue paper or newspaper and store them in a cool dry storage space in single layers with none of them touching. Late-fruiting varieties of pears can be stored in this way; early varieties should be eaten, canned, or frozen. If storage space is limited, cut fruit into rings and dry them in a cool oven (around 200°F or 100°C).

VEGETABLES

Onions and garlic are traditionally braided and hung in an airy shed. To stop bulbs from sprouting, hold the rooted ends over a flame for a few seconds. A good tip is to pour them into old nylon stockings and hang these in a dry shed or garage. Store root vegetables over winter in cool, dry, dark conditions. Wring the tops off carrots, beets, and parsnips rather than cutting them, and store them in layers between sand or dry peat in old galvanized tubs or wooden boxes.

Lay carrots in wooden boxes filled with sand, and store them in a cool dark place.

Pumpkins are a staple ingredient in delicious pies and soups, and are a common feature in Halloween celebrations on October 31st.

PEAR

CHAPTER 5

FRIENDS & FOES

GARDENERS HAVE ALWAYS SHARED THEIR GARDENS WITH OTHER CREATURES. FEW OF US MIND LOSING AN OCCASIONAL PLANT BUT WHEN UNINVITED CREATURES MOVE IN WHOLESALE, IT IS TIME TO ACT. BEFORE YOU REACH FOR A CHEMICAL SOLUTION, STOP TO THINK. MOST CHEMICALS WILL EFFECTIVELY RID YOU OF UNWANTED PESTS AND STOP THE SPREAD OF DISEASES. BUT THEY WILL PROBABLY ALSO HARM LOTS OF CREATURES THAT YOU DO NOT WANT HARMED, AND THEY WILL CERTAINLY DESTROY ANY BALANCE THAT HELPS NATURE TO KEEP THE WORST OF THE PESTS AT BAY.

NOT SURPRISINGLY, SOME OF THE OLD WAYS OF KEEPING UNWELCOME GARDEN VISITORS AT BAY ARE STILL THE BEST. AND A GARDEN WITH BUZZING FRIENDLY INSECTS AND CHIRPING BIRDS GIVES EXTRA JOY.

GARDENERS HAVE ALWAYS COMPLAINED ABOUT
PESTS, BUT SOME INSECTS HAVE ALWAYS BEEN
WELCOMED INTO THE GARDEN, EVEN ENTICED
WITH THEIR FAVORITE FOOD PLANTS. LEARN TO
RECOGNIZE AND ENCOURAGE INSECT FRIENDS.

Insect friends

PREDATORY INSECTS

Very few insects are real pests: some are
pollinators, others decompose waste material,
or are food for birds and fish. Many act as
predators or parasites, killing insects that are
pests. These tigers of the insect world need to
eat other insects to complete their life cycle.
Buy a good insect guide and learn to recognize the insects in your yard.

Ladybugs are a friend
to your garden, as
they prey on insect-
pest aphids.

TIP

• The small flowers of dill,
parsley, catnip, lemon balm,
and thyme provide food for
tiny predator insects that
can drown in the nectar of
larger flowers; daisies
(*Bellis* spp.), coneflowers
(*Echinacea* spp.), and
yarrow (*Achillea millefolium*)
are good pollen sources.
Annuals, such as candytuft
(*Iberis* spp.), marigolds
(*Tagetes* spp.), and salvias
(*Salvia* spp.) also attract.

• Leave areas in the garden
for beneficial insects. Keep
perennial plantings for them
near, or among, the annual
flowers and vegetables.

BEETLES

Sap-sucking aphids are among the most irritating
pests, but they provide food for lots of other insects.
Ladybugs are well-known aphid predators, and
hundreds of other beetles also prey on aphids,
spider mites, and other small pests. Some have gray
or yellow wing covers marked with black spots or
blotches; the spider-mite destroyer is tiny and totally
black. Large, shiny, black groundbeetles eat slug
eggs, grubs, and insect pupae in the soil. Slim and
speedy rove beetles look like earwigs without pin-
cers; they prey on maggots, insect eggs, and grubs
in the soil.

Wasps have their uses: they kill hundreds of flies to feed their young.

TIP

Provide a source of drinking water where insects won't drown. Fill a container of water with stones, so that the stones become islands. Or make a floating island in a pond from a disc of wood.

FLIES AND BUGS

Not all flies are a nuisance. Helpful flies include tiny, delicate aphid midges and yellow-and-black or white-and-black striped hoverflies – both eat thousands of aphids. Lacewings have large, finely veined wings. Their larvae are known as "aphid lions" because they eat so many aphids, along with spider mites, thrips, leafhoppers, small caterpillars, and insect eggs. Assassin and ambush bugs also eat lots of the insects you don't want.

WASPS

Even ordinary garden wasps are excellent predators. They can bring over two hundred flies per hour to a single nest to feed their young, and they pull caterpillars out of your garden. Other welcome wasps, including the ichneumonid wasp, don't sting. They lay their eggs in insect pests including cabbage leaf caterpillars, sawflies, pest beetles, and aphids.

BRINGING THEM HOME

Pollen and nectar plants attract beneficial insects to your yard. The adult beneficial flies, midges, and parasitic wasps must have nectar to give them the energy to lay eggs, whereas ladybugs, lacewings, and pirate bugs supplement their diets with pollen when prey is scarce. Once the adults are attracted to the garden, they are likely to stay and lay their eggs there.

Try adding some of the following nectar-rich plants to your garden to keep the good guys hanging around:

DILL

Buckwheat *(Fagopyrum esculentum)*
Cinquefoil *(Potentilla* spp.*)*
Common yarrow *(Achillea millefolium)*
Cosmos *(Cosmos* spp.*)*
Dill *(Anethum graveolens)*
Fennel *(Foeniculum vulgare)*
Four-wing saltbush *(Atriplex canescens)*
Marigold *(Tagetes* spp.*)*
Poppy mallow *(Callirhoe involucrata)*
Rocky mountain penstemon *(Penstemon strictus)*
Sweet alyssum *(Lobularia maritima)*
Wild bergamot *(Monarda fistulosa)*
Betony *(Stachys officinalis)*
Zinnia *(Zinnia* spp.*)*

ZINNIA

89

SOMETIMES MARAUDING INSECTS DO
CAUSE A REAL PROBLEM IN YOUR GARDEN.
FORTUNATELY THERE ARE PLENTY OF
GARDEN-SAFE WAYS TO TAKE ACTION.

Insects

Every gardener has experienced the joy of waiting for new blossoms, only to be foiled by aphids getting there first. If there are no ladybugs around, try sprinkling powdered garlic over the affected plants, or use garlic spray. Magnesium-rich banana peels on the soil may keep aphids from roses. Lemongrass (*Cymbopogon citratus*) repels them due to the oils it exudes.

DEALING WITH ANTS

Ants are irritating, largely because they protect aphids in order to feed off their honeydew secretions. The traditional remedy is to pour boiling water into ants' nests. This destroys their home so they have to move elsewhere; a small number may drown. To make it more effective add several drops of strong chili pepper sauce to the boiling water; this will be too fiery for them.

CARROT RUST FLY

Carrot rust fly is a persistent nuisance in some gardens. Carrot rust flies hunt by smell, so sprinkle dried aromatic herbs or garlic in the trench with the carrot seed. Parsley or onions sown nearby will also keep carrot rust flies off the scent. Or stop carrot rust flies from getting into your garden by erecting temporary barriers over your carrots with floating row-cover fabric.

MYTH BUSTER

GARLIC

The best solution is to stop insects ever taking a liking to your plants. Ancient wisdom suggests planting a garlic clove beside each of your rose bushes. The garlic bulbs donate excess sulfur to the soil, among other minerals and enzymes that are taken up by the rose, where they act as an effective insect repellent, and also protect roses against black spot. Any member of the allium family will do the trick, and chives are especially attractive planted under roses.

TIP

If you can bear to, leave an ants' nest in the garden. It may attract attractive flying predators, such as woodpeckers, into your garden. Ants are one of their favorite foods.

ROSE BUSH

MYTH BUSTER

Yellow flowers were often planted in vegetable gardens in the belief that this kept insects away. But, in fact, it probably encouraged insects in the garden, because many of them are particularly attracted to yellow. The deterrent effect was probably because it lured them onto the yellow flowers and off the vegetables.

FLEA BEETLE TIPS

These little flying beetles feast on young brassicas, but they navigate by smell. Repel them by mulching plants with elder *(Sambucus* spp.*)* leaves and flowers, or grow strong-smelling herbs such as common wormwood *(Artemisia absinthium)* nearby. They love yellow, so position yellow sticky traps above the plants. Cover seedlings with row-cover fabric or wait to transplant them in mid-summer for a fall crop. The lifecycle of the flea beetle takes them elsewhere by then.

VINE WEEVIL

These are terrible pests. Adults can be trapped on sticky bands because they don't fly, they walk, but grubs are the real pest. Particularly common in container-grown plants, they eat the roots of plants and it's only when plants die that you find out why. Treat vine weevils with commercially available parasitic nematodes.

Protect apple trees from flying insects by hanging a plastic container in the tree, filled with a solution of 1 cup vinegar, 1 cup sugar, and 2 pints water.

Insect attack

SOMETIMES PREVENTION IS NOT ENOUGH AND YOU HAVE TO TAKE ACTION. CHOOSE PEST-SPECIFIC DETERRENTS, BUT IF YOU REALLY DO HAVE TO RESORT TO SPRAYING, CHOOSE NATURAL SOAPS AND SPRAYS.

MYTH BUSTER

Because wireworms attack potatoes, some old gardening books suggested you could attract and trap them by leaving old potato peelings lying on your soil. In fact, you must bury the bait. Punch holes in old food cans, fill them with potato peelings, and bury them in the soil. Empty cans once a week and replace the bait as necessary.

WIREWORM TRAP

REPEL AND ATTRACT

Some plants keep pests away. No cottage gardener would have planted cabbages or carrots without sage *(Salvia officinalis)* or thyme *(Thymus officinalis)* nearby. Insects such as carrot rust fly locate their food by smell, so strong-scented herbs keep them away. Catnip *(Nepeta cataria)*, tansy *(Tanacetum vulgare)*, and marigolds *(Tagetes* spp.*)* keep cucumber beetles away, and mosquitoes hate eucalyptus *(Eucalyptus* spp.*)*, lemon geraniums *(Pelargonium odoratissimum)*, mint *(Mentha* spp.*)*, and rosemary *(Rosmarinus officinalis)*. But some plants are irresistible to pests, so traditional gardeners planted them just to keep bugs off of other crops. Aphids are attracted to nasturtiums *(Tropaeolum majus)*, which lure the pests away from other tasty fruits and vegetables. Sowthistle *(Sonchus* spp.*)* lures aphids.

Modern gardeners can go one step further and lure bugs with the promise of sex. Pheromones are chemicals released by females to attract males, and scientists have developed synthetic chemicals to give the same signals, luring unsuspecting adult males into a sticky trap or a container with no exit. Pheromone traps control a variety of pests including Japanese beetles, fruit flies, gypsy moths, codling moths, and corn borers.

When you plant a new area of your garden that was grass, watch out for wireworms. They eat roots and the underground parts of stems. Wireworms are larvae of the click beetle; they take from three to five years to finish their cycle and fly away. Until they turn into flying beetles, they feed underground.

NASTURTIUMS

⟳ Pick aphids off plant leaves and stems, and squash them between your thumb and little finger. Or spray them with soapy water.

MYTH BUSTER

Elder leaves were a common cure-all in folk medicine. They include similar chemical compounds to foxgloves *(Digitalis* spp.*)*, and many myths surrounding them are the same. Tea made from 1 lb (450 g) elder leaves to 6 pt (3 L) water helps plants build up their own immunity, repelling pests and diseases.

CABBAGE WHITE CATERPILLAR

SPRAY AWAY

Before insecticides, people used what was available. Soap has always been a standby, because repeated spraying with soapy water deters most insects. Most household soaps, however, can harm the leaves of plants. Purchase "insecticidal soap," specially formulated so it does not harm plants. Many deterrent sprays can be made from kitchen-cupboard ingredients like baking soda and salt, or by using solutions of crushed plants.

Choose natural insecticidal soap for aphids, blackfly, whitefly, and scale insects and confine treatments to the plants being damaged. Aphids and spider mites can also be dislodged with a strong spray of water from a garden hose.

PICK YOUR OWN

When you see aphids, blackfly, and greenfly, either wash them off plants or pick them off and squash them between your finger and thumb. Caterpillars, such as the striped cabbage worms, which feast on brassicas and decimate verbascum, should be picked off, put in a bucket and drowned, or fed to fowl. Whitefly descend in clouds on plants; pick and vacuum off the worst of them; then spray the rest with elder tea (see page 109).

CANNIBAL TEA

Earwigs are not much of a pest except in dry soils. It was once suggested that gardeners should stir their nests regularly to "harass them to death." It's easier to trap them by leaving cardboard tubes on the ground overnight. Collect the tubes in the morning, empty out the earwigs and drown them in a bucket of water. Add beetles, slugs, and snails, steep the lot for a few days, strain the bodies out onto the compost heap, and use the liquid as an insect repellent. It smells foul but works well. Biodynamic gardeners collect and burn the bodies of pests, spreading their ashes as a pest-deterrent during specific.

AS LONG AS THERE HAVE BEEN GARDENS THERE
HAVE BEEN SLUGS AND SNAILS, SO GARDENERS
HAVE DEVELOPED MANY FAVORITE METHODS TO
KEEP THEM OFF THE PLANTS.

Slugs & snails

Fortunately, there are some tried and tested methods of deterring snails and slugs, but you may need to try several to find the best way for you and your garden.

THISTLE

DETER SLUGS AND SNAILS

Every gardener has been troubled by slugs and snails at some time. Before you see the tell-tale signs of nibbled plants, you see their slimy trails. Slugs are soft-bodied mollusks, moving along on slime that contains chemical information to help them navigate. Snails are little more than slugs with shells on. Their favorite snacks are juicy young shoots emerging from the ground in spring, and tender young seedlings, but they will eat virtually anything.

Soft slimy bodies and hard sharp substances do not mix, so the best way to deter slugs is to lay gritty barriers. A 17th century saying suggests the following method for deterring slugs: "If horsehair rope is laid abroad your bed, slugs cannot feed but wound themselves instead." If you ever sat on a horsehair-stuffed sofa, you would know how prickly it can be. Chopped thistles, gorse clippings, and barley husks were also highly recommended.

MODERN BARRIER METHODS

Sawdust is usually easy to come by for free and it makes a
good barrier; crushed shells and sand also work because when
a slug or snail crosses it, it cuts its body and kills it.

If your soil is very light and you don't want to make it even
lighter, you can buy diatomaceous earth, which includes many
tiny razor-sharp fossilized remains. Bran is a cheap and
effective barrier which ultimately breaks down to make a good
soil conditioner. As slugs and snails cross a bran barrier it
leaches moisture from them, and if they eat any it swells up
inside them so they die. All barrier methods need to be
reapplied after rain.

HOSTA

Place a collar of aluminum foil on
the ground around favorite plants
to keep slugs and snails away.

METAL DETECTORS

In 1849, a manual "containing methods for
destroying all kinds of vermin and insects
injurious to the garden" recommended
"galvanic protectors." These were shortened
cones of zinc sheet metal with a strip of
copper on the outer surface; apparently any
slugs attempting to crawl over them would
receive a "galvanic shock." Try aluminum foil
collars around plants for the same effect.
Strips of copper also appear to stop slugs
in their tracks.

IF BARRIERS LOOK
OUT OF PLACE IN
YOUR GARDEN, YOU
CAN TRAP SLUGS, OR
ENCOURAGE OTHER
LIVING CREATURES
TO GET RID OF THEM
FOR YOU.

Slug traps

One highly effective method is to mount evening slug hunts
using a flashlight. Patrol your garden with a bucket to collect as
many as you can, then kill them: drown them in hot water, crush
them, pour salt on them, or feed them to ducks. This is a job
that children love, and if you offer them a price per slug or snail
you'll be surprised how many they'll find!

SLUG PATROL

⟳ Toads love to eat
slugs. Make your
garden toad-
friendly with a
source of water
and some dark,
damp places for
them to hide.

MYTH BUSTER

Some old gardeners swore by water traps,
making a watery barrier on the edge of beds.
Slugs and snails are reluctant swimmers, so
it is easy to pick them out of the water if they
fall in. But unless your watery moat is deep
and solid, slugs will burrow into the bed from
elsewhere, and the population may even
increase as it is harder for them to get out
and move elsewhere.

OTHER CREATURES CAN HELP

Encourage birds by putting up nesting boxes and planting shrubs with dense foliage. Thrushes and blackbirds particularly love snails, crushing their shells on a hard stone to get at the creatures. Frogs and hedgehogs adore slugs, so do toads. Make a pond, even a tiny one, introduce frogs, and include some damp, dark hiding places for toads to live. Ducks also find slugs tasty and some beetles dine on slugs' and snails' eggs – don't tidy up your garden too much but leave a few logs and stones for beetle homes.

MYTH BUSTER

A favorite traditional slug trap uses a cabbage leaf pinned down over some orange peel to entice slugs under, in the belief that slugs are attracted to citrus fruit. Upturned grapefruit halves are also popular. There is no evidence that citrus exudations attract slugs more than any other vegetation. These traps only work by providing a moist and shady environment for slugs. They are just as likely to gather in a bed full of leafy greens or other tasty shady places.

Old jam jars make a perfect beer trap. Sink a jar half full of beer into the ground and the unsuspecting slugs will be drawn in. Remember to give other insects an escape route by leaving in a twig or two.

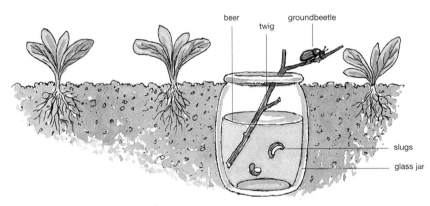

beer   twig   groundbeetle

slugs

glass jar

TRAPS AND DECOYS

Like so many creatures, slugs are attracted to beer, and sinking jars half full of beer at strategic points in your garden should encourage slugs to head for these beer traps rather than your plants. Or make decoys from small piles of chopped-up juicy lettuce or comfrey leaves to provide slugs and snails with pre-planned meals. Place them as far away as possible from the crops you are trying to protect, or you'll find the pests just move on to your other plants for dessert.

TIP

Use beer traps only until early summer, when bees head for them. You don't want to end up drowning bees too. Leave a couple of twigs in the jar so that groundbeetles have a way to climb out.

BIOLOGICAL CONTROL

Increasingly, serious gardeners are turning to biological control. You can buy microscopic parasites called nematodes to put into the soil. They enter the slug's or snail's body and multiply inside it so that their host swells to a size where it no longer feeds, then burrows deep into the ground and dies. Biological control works best in a controlled environment, such as a greenhouse, where soil conditions and temperature are reasonably constant.

WHILE FEW PEOPLE WOULD SEEK A GARDEN COMPLETELY FREE OF WILDLIFE, THERE ARE SOME FOUR-LEGGED CREATURES THAT ARE DEFINITELY NOT WELCOME.

Four-legged pests

Knowing and spotting your culprits is the first step in any sensible method of pest control in the garden. The easiest and surest means of identification is to catch the pest in the act. Animals can also be identified by footprints, manure, fur, and habits. Once you know what pest you are dealing with, you can figure out how best to approach the problem. How does it get into the garden? Does it walk, climb, or burrow? Will more follow? How much damage is it likely to do and does it need to be controlled?

DON'T ENCOURAGE PESTS

You can't help it if moles and gophers move in, it just means you have good underground supplies of food. But most mammals probably find your garden strictly by chance. While out foraging for meals they find something they like, so they come back, often until it is all gone. So if you see where they have been munching, a first step is to try to deter them by making their food unpalatable.

Raccoons are a major pest in many North American gardens, so try to fence them out.

○ Deer can be relentless and greedy trespassers in suburban gardens if you grow plants or young trees that they like to eat.

○ Although they look cute, moles are a pest in the garden, as they uproot plants and destroy lawns. See page 100 for a variety of deterrents.

See page 100 for a variety of deterrents.

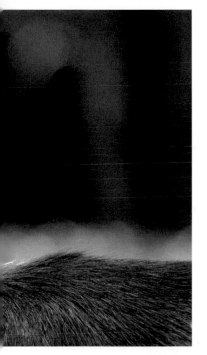

MYTH BUSTER

In the 18th century, a popular gardening manual suggested the best way to make moles leave a garden: "Take red herrings and cutting them in pieces; burn the pieces on the molehills, or put garlicke or leeks in the mouths of their Hill and the mole will leave the ground."

CATMINT

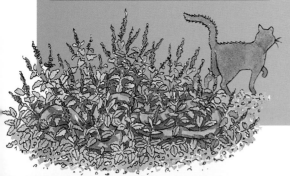

Animal attraction

Seaweed seems to attract many mammals, from deer to squirrels, into gardens. Rotting seaweed on the surface of a bed may also attract unwelcome flies. But this doesn't mean you can't use it as a great all-purpose soil conditioner. Just make sure you dig it in right away or compost it, or make it into liquid fertilizer.

In urban gardens, catmint (*Nepeta cataria*) may attract unwelcome cats. It's not a good idea to repel other people's domestic pets with noxious substances, so try the old trick of winding lengths of hose or rope in plants or beds. Apparently it looks like snakes and keeps them out.

Rabbits adore dill, so if you can't keep them out of your garden, plant dill near the edge and hope that they stop there rather than moving on to other plants.

Many animals, including deer, raccoons, foxes, and badgers forage by night. You can keep them off your patch by making it seem occupied. If it won't disturb your neighbors, you could rig up lights or sounds that go on or off during the night.

Don't leave a music station on the radio at night to deter nocturnal animals. They seem to like music – but you might try a talk radio station instead!

IF YOU STILL HAVE
A PROBLEM WITH
ANIMALS RAIDING
YOUR PATCH, MOVE
ON TO MORE SPECIFIC
REMEDIES.

More mammals

MOLES AND GOPHERS

Moles and gophers are very good at aerating the soil in your garden, but in the process they wreak havoc. Heaps of earth appear all over your garden at miraculous speed, plants are uprooted, and lawns destroyed.

The caper spurge *(Euphorbia lathyrus)* is sometimes known as gopher plant because gophers supposedly avoid it. It smells strongly and contains poisonous alkaloids. However, if your mole or gopher population is large, you will have to have massed plantings of caper spurge.

WHIRLIGIG

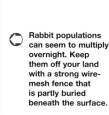

Rabbit populations can seem to multiply overnight. Keep them off your land with a strong wire-mesh fence that is partly buried beneath the surface.

TIP

Before the days of bagged composts and soil conditioners, gardeners used the loose soil pushed up by moles and gophers for potting their plants.

DETERRENTS

If the tunnels are not in the garden, try burying used cat litter or dog dirt, or even human or animal hair at the end of a mole or gopher run; they may think there are predators and flee. Moles and gophers hate vibrations, so you could try placing children's whirligigs in the most recently turned earth, moving them back along the run until the moles have disappeared. Or use half-filled bottles partly buried in the ground so the wind can whistle across their tops and make an irritating noise.

Mice love to eat seeds and bulbs, preventing a colorful display later in the year. Put them off by dipping the seeds in paraffin.

MICE

Mice are a pest in the garden, because they eat seeds and bulbs. Old-fashioned gardeners dip pea and bean seeds in paraffin before planting them, as mice hate the taste and smell. To prevent them from eating bulbs stored in the shed, sprinkle the bulbs with talcum powder. If you have very chalky soil, rinse them before planting, as talcum powder adds to the calcium levels.

Plant rue *(Ruta graveolens)* strategically around your garden to ward off stray dogs, as they will hate the scent.

BARRIER FENCE

Step 1
Dig trench in front of posts.

Step 2
Bury wire mesh fence 8 in (20 cm) in the trench and backfill.

Step 3
Attach fence firmly to posts with staples.

SCENT-SENSITIVE

The worst thing about rabbits is that they breed so rapidly; a minor problem can quickly reach epidemic proportions. Rabbits are very shy of humans and sensitive to smell, and an old trick was to put 18 in (45 cm) tall forked sticks around the perimeter of your garden with tufts of human hair attached. The only sure-fire way to keep rabbits out – or raccoons – is to erect a strong wire-mesh fence with 12-18 in (30-45 cm) firmly buried under the soil.

Deer can also be kept from a garden by the scent of deodorant soap hung around the perimeter. Keep cats off beds by removing all traces of their smell – lay scented herbs over the areas where they mess, then plant short sharp sticks in the ground to keep them from using your beds as litter boxes.

Dogs hate the scent of rue *(Ruta graveolens)*, so you could try planting a few bushes at possible entrance points.

TIP

Leave the top 10 in (25 cm) of any fence loose, so climbing creatures can't get over it easily.

MYTH BUSTER

An old trick to prevent mice from stealing your pea seeds was to bury gorse *(Ulex europaeus)* and holly *(Ilex spp.)* clippings in the sowing trenches. However, this is not recommended today as these both make the soil rather acid where they decompose. If you have a serious mouse problem in your garden, it is best to sow peas in late spring.

FRUIT TREES, SOFT FRUIT, AND SEEDS ARE
PARTICULARLY VULNERABLE TO ATTACK
BY BIRDS, BUT BECAUSE BIRDS CAN ALSO BE
GREAT FRIENDS TO ANY GARDENER, CHOOSE
FRIENDLY METHODS OF CONTROL.

CROW

Birds

Scarecrows were once a common sight in fields and gardens. They can be very effective.

You should welcome birds, because they eat slugs and snails, and other pests – and they aerate the soil where they pierce it with their beaks to seek insects. They can also look and sound beautiful. However, they relish seeds, young flowers, and fruit of all sorts, so you may need to keep them off parts of your garden.

SCARING BIRDS

Scarecrows aren't too popular today, but dress a figure in red clothes and it will keep the birds away. For extra effect, hang discs of aluminum foil from its head and limbs so they move and jangle in the breeze. If jays and magpies are a pest, hang small plastic flowerpots instead as they are attracted by shiny objects.

Metal wind chimes work well among soft fruit bushes, or tie small metal rods onto pieces of twine so they bump together in the slightest breeze. Lengths of twine with brightly colored plastic or foil strips also work well.

HOMEMADE
BIRDSCARER

TIP

When sowing special seeds that must not end up as bird feed, try this old remedy. Boil a handful of wheat and barley seeds in wine; let it steep. Mix the strained solution with a spoon of powdered sneeze-wort root (*Achillea ptarmica*). Water around the seedbed with the liquid and birds should stay away.

TIP

• Net individual fruits or bunches of fruit with old nylon stockings and tights, and nut and fruit nets.

• Plant blackberry bushes and wild roses among your fruit trees. Birds will choose the blackberries and rose-hips rather than attacking your fall fruit. Plant insect-attracting plants, such as bee balm *(Monarda didyma)* on the edge of fruit beds, so the birds will be tempted to feed off insects rather than berries.

You will have to net a cherry tree – or make a web of thread – to get the fruit before the birds do.

PROTECTING TREES

Net cherry and mulberry trees if you want to harvest any fruit, or create a web of strong black thread between the branches. Nylon-based thread is strong, but difficult to remove and can cut into the branches if it is not removed as trees grow. Birds find it difficult to judge the distance between the threads and tend to avoid them. Mirrors hung in trees are also effective – if birds catch sight of themselves they are often frightened away.

MYTH BUSTER

Birds don't like strong-smelling herbs, such as lavender or sage, so gardeners can safely plant the bright colored primulas, polyanthus, and crocus, which birds otherwise adore, in their vicinity. But don't use this companion planting for strawberries, which will fail in the company of plants that give off strong-smelling oils.

SUCCESSFUL SOWING

"One for the rook, one for the crow, one to spoil and one to grow." Crows have great eyesight. Don't let them see you plant corn and don't leave any seeds exposed. Birds are fond of grass seeds, so cover the ground in a small area with a criss-cross of black thread held about 3 in (8 cm) off the ground by sticks. In a large area the best way is to sow extra seeds.

When sowing vegetables, keep birds off by covering the rows with simple cloches made of chicken wire, or try the ancient method of sticking a few feathers into halved potatoes. Lay a few of the potato halves between the rows. Birds avoid them, presumably because they resemble dead birds.

BEES, BUTTERFLIES, AND SOME BIRDS ARE VITAL POLLINATORS IN YOUR GARDEN. ENCOURAGE THEM TO VISIT AND STAY BY CREATING PLACES FOR THEM TO LIVE AND BY GROWING THEIR PREFERRED PLANTS.

Pollinators

BEES

Bees are an integral part of a healthy garden. The earlier the honey bees get to work, the more pollen they collect, the more honey they make, and the better the yields from your well-pollinated fruit and vegetables. "A swarm of bees in May is worth a load of hay. A swarm of bees in June is worth a silver spoon. A swarm of bees in July isn't worth a fly."

Bees need continuous supplies of pollen; they happily forage in fields, orchards, and hedgerows. Their favorite garden flowers include aconites (*Aconitum* spp.), cornflowers (*Montana* spp.), lavender (*Lavandula* spp.), catmint (*Nepeta* spp.), and scabiosa (*Scabiosa* spp.).

Every garden needs bees to pollinate trees, flowers, and vegetables.

A monarch butterfly hovers over a geranium.

HUMMINGBIRDS

Long before the common honeybee was brought to North America as a pollinator, hummingbirds were busy. These tiny birds need to consume more than half their weight in food each day, visiting hundreds of flowers each day and feasting on insects So they are not only efficient pollinators but also pest predators.

Unlike butterflies, hummingbirds are attracted to flower colors and nectar, not fragrance. Your hummingbirds may become reliant on your garden for food, and there may be periods when there are no blossoms for nectar. So hang hummingbird feeders about 30 ft (9 m) apart throughout your garden for these times. Choose bright red feeders to attract the birds from a distance.

Hummingbirds are attracted to brightly colored plants.

Favorite Hummingbird flowers

Abelia (*Abelia grandiflora*)
Azalea (*Rhododendron* spp.)
Butterfly bush (*Buddleia davidii*)
Eucalyptus (*Eucalyptus* spp.)
Fuchsia tree (*Fuchsia arborescens*)
Hibiscus (*Hibiscus* spp.)
Lilac (*Syringa* spp.)
Four o'clocks (*Mirabilis jalapa*)
Flowering tobacco (*Nicotiana alata*)
Nasturtium (*Tropaeolum majus*)
Petunia (*Petunia hybrida*)
Spider flower (*Cleome hasslerana*)
Zinnia (*Zinnia* spp.)
Bee balm (*Monarda didyma*)
Butterfly weed (*Ascelpias tuberosa*)
Cardinal flower (*Lobelia cardinalis*)
Columbine (*Aquilegia* spp.)
Cosmos (*Cosmos* spp.)
Dahlia (*Dahlia* spp.)
Delphinium (*Delphinium elatum*)

ABELIA

HIBISCUS

Artist's acanthus (*Acanthus mollis*)
Foxglove (*Digitalis purpurea*)
Fuchsia (*Fuchsia hybrida*)
Geranium (*Pelargonium* spp.)
Monkey flower (*Mimulus hybridus*)
Penstemon (*Penstemon* spp.)
Red hot poker (*Kniphofia uvaria*)
Sage (*Salvia officinalis*)
Verbena (*Verbena* spp.)
Cardinal climber (*Ipomoea quamoclit*)
Honeysuckle (*Lonicera* spp.)
Lantana (*Lantana* spp.)
Chinese creeper (*Campsis grandiflora*)
Trumpet vines (*Bignonia tagliabuana*)

ALL COUNTRY GARDENS USED TO HAVE A POND, EVEN IF IT WAS ONLY A SINK SUBMERGED IN THE GROUND. THEY PROVIDE A HOME AND FOOD AND DRINK FOR MANY GARDEN FRIENDS.

Pond life

Ponds are a magnet to wildlife, and they don't need to be large or deep. Frogs and toads will be happy with something only puddle-sized, and they do nothing but good in your garden. It is also great fun for adults and children to bring frog eggs home and watch the tadpoles hatch and grow into frogs. Frogs and toads eat slugs and snails, flies, and other pests.

Waterlily flowers, pads, and varied marginal plants make an ideal watery habitat.

MYTH BUSTER

People used to think that toads could give you warts; but warts are caused by a virus. This common myth probably originated because many toads have bumps on their skin that look like warts. These bumps contain poison that irritates the mouth of any predator that tries to eat a toad, and can cause convulsions in humans. Take care if handling toads and always wash your hands afterward.

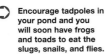

Encourage tadpoles in your pond and you will soon have frogs and toads to eat the slugs, snails, and flies.

TIP

Toads and frogs burrow under plant material in the winter, or under upturned flowerpots. Make them hiding places by upturning clay flowerpots over a stone or two to allow access. A slightly elevated flat rock also makes a cool, shady toad home.

CLEARING BLANKET WEED

Step 1
If left unchecked, blanket weed can choke a pond. If you have ducks, they'll clear it; otherwise, remove the weeds with a bamboo cane.

Step 2
Hold it in the pond where the weed is thickest, then twist and pull, and the weed will cover the cane like spaghetti on a fork.

Step 3
Pull out the cane and deposit the weed beside the pond for a day, so any trapped pondlife can crawl out. Then put the weed on your compost heap.

TIP

When starting a pond, fill it with tap water and let it stand for at least a day so all the chlorine evaporates. If transferring tadpoles, toad eggs, or fish from another pond, bring them in a bucket full of water from their original home, and leave the bucket in the new pond for several hours with the rim just below the water level, so the waters gradually mix.

BEST SITES FOR A POND

A pond is best sited in a quiet corner of the garden, ideally partly in sun but partly shaded. A couple of inches of soil on the bottom will encourage aquatic insects to breed. In a pond larger than 6 ft (2 m) diameter, aquatic plants such as water lilies provide shelter for many creatures. Baby frogs love to emerge and sit on them; water snails, which help clean ponds, lay their eggs on the undersurface.

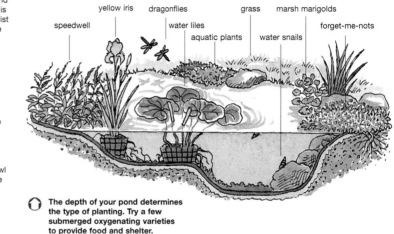

The depth of your pond determines the type of planting. Try a few submerged oxygenating varieties to provide food and shelter.

PLANTS

Plant a few submerged oxygenating plants to provide food and shelter for tadpoles and larvae, and to keep the pond clean. Allow them to grow thickly in some parts, but keep a few areas clear once they have become established. Marginal plants such as yellow iris *(Iris pseudacorus)* are favored by dragonflies, which eat huge numbers of insect pests. Marsh marigolds *(Caltha palustris)* have attractive flowers early in spring, and their large leaves provide shelter for newts and other pond life; speedwell *(Veronica spp.)* and forget-me-nots *(Myosotis palustris)* grow out from the banks in floating mats for cover. Floating plants help to cut down the amount of sunlight entering the water and so control algae.

FISH

Ornamental fish are very attractive in ponds, but if you want other pond life, don't have too many fish in a small pond or they'll eat all the tadpoles and larvae. Fish may attract visitors, such as herons and raccoons. To keep predators from eating the fish, stretch a network of fine black wire about 8 in (20 cm) above the pond.

Don't let too many leaves fall into your pond or they will choke the oxygen, and pond creatures will die. In late summer, lay some fine-gauge wire mesh or bird netting over the pond to catch the leaves, and remove them before they rot.

PLANTS, JUST LIKE HUMANS, CAN SUFFER FROM A RANGE OF ILLNESSES CAUSED BY BACTERIA, VIRUSES, AND ALSO FUNGAL INFECTIONS. BUT MOST DISEASES CAN BE PREVENTED WITH GOOD HUSBANDRY.

Diseases

HEALTHY PLANTING

The best way to keep your plants pest- and disease-free is to cultivate healthy soil and give plants the conditions they need. Do not plant too closely together, keep your soil well fertilized and your plants well nourished. Be careful about garden hygiene: make sure your compost is stored under cover, and that your pots are not contaminated with old soil or plant fragments. Also, make sure your garden tools are sharp and clean.

COMBAT DISEASE

Most diseases – except powdery mildew – spread more easily in the wet, so don't work on plants in wet weather. If you do find any diseased plants, uproot them and trash or burn them. Never compost diseased plants. Many viral diseases are spread by sucking insects, so control of your insect population should keep plants fairly virus-free. Where possible, buy disease-resistant varieties such as rust-resistant hollyhocks (Althea rosea) or mosaic-virus-resistant cucumbers.

MYTH BUSTER

Several books mention a cure of hanging mothballs on a peach tree to prevent peach leaf curl. This assumes that peach leaf curl is spread by insects and the mothballs deter them. But mothballs are toxic, and peach leaf curl is in fact a fungus, which is most active in cool and rainy springs. Peach leaf curl can be easily prevented by planting peach and almond trees against walls where you can erect temporary shelters in winter and remove them in summer.

HOLLYHOCK

TIP

When using recycled pots, wash them out in a bath of 9 parts water to 1 part bleach to kill any fungus and bacteria.

PROTECTING PEACH TREES

Step 1
Cut a strip of wood wider than your peach tree. Attach a couple of hooks to the ends. Fix the strip on the wall above the tree.

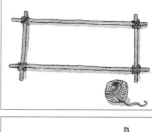

Step 2
Cut four strips of bamboo and bind the ends of the the strips together with string.

Step 3
Place a plastic sheet over the frame, tuck over the ends, and staple together.

Step 4
Cut bamboo strips the height of the wooden strip and bind to the frame with string. Hook the frame onto the strip of wood.

Peach trees will thrive in even cool, damp climates if they are protected from spring rains.

TIP

• Damping-off disease is common in cooler climates where you must start seeds indoors. This fungal disease, sclerotina, causes seedlings to rot at soil level. Prevent it by keeping air circulating around your seed trays and spread a fine layer of milled sphagnum moss on the surface of the flats. Sclerotina fungus thrives in wet soil, so never overwater your seedlings.

• Never spray a plant late in the day. It must dry out before evening, because damp foliage on a cool night attracts pests and diseases.

TRADITIONAL CURE-ALLS

Burying sticks of rhubarb in sowing or planting holes is an ancient method of controlling clubroot in cabbages. Rhubarb contains oxalic acid that deters the enzymes that cause clubroot.

Onion juice or garlic tea are traditional fungicidal and bactericidal remedies, and good general pest and disease cure-alls (see next pages). Use as a spray to control greenfly and aphids as well as to alleviate black spot on roses. As a cure for mildew on brassicas, try a spray of diluted cider vinegar (see page 111).

Compost tea is made by steeping half a bucket of well-rotted compost in water for two or three days. It seems to be one of the best tonics for plants stressed by insects or fungal diseases. Strain and dilute it to an amber color, then drench the plant's leaves with it. Elder tea is another powerful cure-all, made from steeping a handful of elder plant (Sambucus spp.) leaves in a jug of boiling water.

BEFORE CHEMICAL SPRAYS, GARDENERS HAD A RANGE
OF KITCHEN-CUPBOARD AND GARDEN-SHED REMEDIES
IF DISEASES COULD NOT BE PREVENTED.

Recipes for control

TRADITIONAL SPRAYS

Your soil is healthy, your plants aren't overcrowded, everything's getting enough food and water, and still there are signs of disease? Sometimes you have no alternative but to spray. Use any of the recipes below, or a combination. Once you've tried traditional sprays you'll wonder why anyone uses chemical controls. Unlike chemicals, you can't overdose with natural sprays: they cannot harm other plants or wildlife; they leave no harmful residues; and they cost little or nothing. Most of these sprays are also useful against insect pests.

HORSETAIL SPRAY

Horsetail (*Equisetum* spp.) is a mineral-rich weed, which helps other plants in all sorts of ways: in compost, as a fertilizer, and general tonic and cure-all. Either dose plants regularly with horsetail tea, made from horsetail steeped in a bath of water for several weeks, or use a quickly prepared and more concentrated remedy. Chop several handfuls of horsetail finely, put into 2 pt (1 L) of water, bring to a boil, and simmer for two to three hours. Cool, strain, and use as spray against mildew and black spot on roses.

ELDER SPRAY

Steep elder leaves (*Sambucus* spp.) in water, or chop leaves and stalks finely and boil like horsetail. Elder has antibacterial as well as fungicidal properties.

ELDER

BRACKEN SPRAY

The leaves of bracken (*Pteridium* spp.) contain an acid that acts against diseases. It is also a good all-purpose soil conditioner because it breaks down fast, releasing many valuable minerals as well as organic matter. Chopped green bracken leaves make a good fungicidal spray, prepared in the same way as horsetail, but don't use them late in the season after they set spores.

BRACKEN

Onion and garlic are antibacterial and antifungal. They also make useful insecticides.

GARLIC SPRAY

Crush a large garlic bulb into 2 pt (1 L) of cold water. Boil for five minutes and allow to cool. Strain and spray as a fungicide and insecticide.

ONION JUICE

Soak a large bunch of onion leaves in a bucket of water for a few days. Strain the liquid and spray it liberally over plants every two weeks to prevent mildew, or on infected plants twice weekly.

SPRAY GUN

BAKING SODA SPRAY

Baking soda spray is an excellent fungicide. Mix 2 tbsp of baking soda in 4 pt (2 L) of water and spray as necessary on problem areas.

ANTIRUST BAKING SODA SPRAY

Make baking soda spray as above but add 3 tbsp of horticultural oil and 1 tbsp of liquid seaweed. Spray this generously onto plants as soon as signs of rust appear.

BAKING SODA

VINEGAR SPRAY

This is another great cupboard spray to combat many fungal diseases. Mix 2 tbsp of cider vinegar in 4 pt (2 L) of water and spray on infected plants in the morning and early evening.

Horsetail is an ancient plant that was alive at the time of the dinosaurs. It mines deep into the subsoil for minerals, which it passes to others in compost or spray.

VINEGAR

TRADITIONAL GARDENERS DIDN'T HASTEN TO UPROOT
EVERY WEED, SO BEFORE YOU RUSH TO ERADICATE
EVERY UNWANTED PLANT IN YOUR GARDEN, PAUSE TO
SEE IF ANY DESERVE TO STAY.

Weeds

WHAT ARE WEEDS?

Walt Whitman called weeds "plants whose virtues have yet to be discovered," but most people define weeds as "plants growing in the wrong place." There are a handful of invaders that really are nothing but trouble, but not all. Weeds colonize disturbed soil, including freshly turned beds. They have little respect for the gardener's desire for an artificial ecosystem. New weeds are constantly arriving, plus fresh supplies of old ones.

WEED FOOD

Dandelions *(Taraxacum officinale)*, Queen Anne's lace *(Anthriscus sylvestris)*, lamb's-quarters *(Chenopodium album),* and black mustard *(Brassica nigra)* provide food and living quarters for helpful insects. Many weeds are also good for us to eat.

Before lemons were widely available, vitamin C-rich sorrel *(Ruimex acetosa)* sauce was often eaten with fish. Try it in salad, perhaps with chickweed *(Stellaria media),* which contains high levels of copper. Blanched young dandelions, or steamed lamb's-quarters are also full of nutritious minerals and vitamins.

Dandelion seeds are attached to tiny parachutes that spread them far and wide.

LAMB'S-QUARTERS

SORREL

MYTH BUSTER

Horsetail (*Equisetum* spp.*)* is so good at mining that it takes up whatever minerals that are in the area, not just soil nutrients. Once, a researcher found a visible amount of gold in the ash of a large crop of horsetail. It also secretes useful amounts of cobalt, calcium, and silica, which are effective against mildews and other fungal diseases. Horsetail tea makes an excellent fungicidal foliar spray (see page 110).

COMPANIONS TO COMPOST

Lamb's-quarters (Chenopodium album) makes a good neighbor because, like nettles, black medics (Medicago lupulina), docks (Rumex spp.) and horsetails (Equisetum spp.), it mines for minerals for other plants to enjoy. Also, its leaf spread catches and carries water to shorter neighbors.

Remedies

Horsetail is useful in clearing polluted soils, especially in cases of heavy metal pollution. Never compost horsetail that's been used in this way but burn it and dispose of the ash away from your garden, as it will contain heavy metal residues.

Plantain (Plantago major) can be an effective treatment for poison ivy rash. Crush plantain leaves and apply them over the affected areas as a poultice. It's not a miracle cure, but helpful if you aren't near a drugstore. It's wise to consult a physician before using herbal remedies.

BLACK MUSTARD

WEED AS FRIEND

Before artificial fertilizers, gardeners knew to compost weeds or make them into teas or washes. Dry deep-rooted perennial weeds such as docks (Rumex spp.) in the sun before composting them, so there is no danger of them rooting in your compost. Tea made from boiling and steeping leaves of black mustard (Brassica nigra) deters cabbage butterflies from laying their eggs.

Some weeds attract pests and can be used as decoy plants. Flea beetles love horsenettle (Solanum carolinense), but destroy it after flowering. It is a member of the tomato family and serves as host to several pepper and tomato viruses. Thistles (Cirsium spp.) attract blackflies and keep them off your beans.

PLANTAIN

THISTLE

WHEN WEEDS
COMPETE WITH
CULTIVATED PLANTS
FOR LIGHT, WATER,
AND NUTRIENTS, THEY
BECOME A REAL
NUISANCE. THEN YOU
NEED TO FOLLOW
TRIED-AND-TESTED
STRATEGIES TO RID
THEM FROM YOUR
GARDEN.

More weeds

Hoe

Bindweed is one of the most difficult weeds to eradicate. You must dig out every segment of root with a fork.

TIP

• When you bring in new perennial plants, check the roots for pieces of weed root, or stem such as bindweed (Convolvulus arvensis) or ground elder (Aegopodium podagraria). This could save a lot of weeding later.

• To get plants going in a very weedy garden, build raised beds and fill them with fresh soil and manure while mulching other areas.

GOOD WEEDING

To keep your garden weed-free, practice good soil management and cultivation, but you may still have some unwanted residents. Hand weeding is often appropriate, but remember the old adage "Pull wet and hoe dry." Weeds are easiest to pull out in wet conditions, but if you hoe in the wet you encourage weeds to spread when you cut their tops off. Annual weeds are best controlled with a mulch or by repeated shallow cultivation in the spring and by keeping them from going to seed in the fall.

You can reduce the vigor of annual weeds by chopping them back, but watch your timing. "Cut thistles in May, they grow in a day. Cut them in June, that is too soon. Cut them in July, then they die." If you cut in early summer it spurs plants to further growth; wait until they are putting their energies into seed production.

Plants need light to grow. Oldtime gardeners used layers of bracken (Pteridium spp.) to suppress persistent weeds. Cover an area with black plastic or cardboard for a year, or peg a heavy natural fiber carpet just over the weeds, leaving it to rot slowly over two or three seasons. Never use hay or straw as weed mulch as these often contain weed seeds that can create a whole new problem.

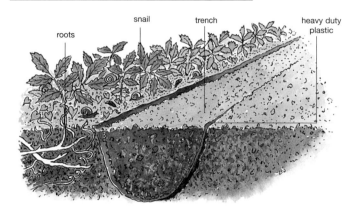

roots — snail — trench — heavy duty plastic

CREEPING ROOTS

Bindweed (*Convolvulus arvensis*), quack/couch grass (*Agropyron repens*), and bishop's weed or ground elder (*Aegopodium podagraria*) spread with a vast network of underground creeping roots. Eradicate them by tilling several times in spring, bringing the rhizomes to the surface where they will dry out and die. Watch out: any tiny segment of root left behind or broken will develop into a new plant – to be sure, smother a badly infested area with mulch.

To prevent weeds from a neighboring yard getting into your garden, dig a trench around 12 in (30 cm) deep around your border and line it with heavy duty plastic. If you keep perennial weeds at bay, this also helps the slug and snail problem, because the pests tend to hide in these weeds and come out at night.

INHIBIT GROWTH

The roots of quack grass (*Agropyron repens*) release chemicals into the soil to inhibit the growth of other plants. So rather than tilling, plant tomatoes. They release enzymes from their roots that inhibit quack grass. Choose a strong-growing variety, such as 'Broad Ripple Yellow Currant'. Sowing turnip seeds among the grass is another traditional remedy.

TOMATOES

CHAPTER 6

THE INDOOR GARDEN

HOUSEPLANTS HAVE A RELATIVELY RECENT HISTORY, BECAUSE THEY NEED MORE LIGHT THAN OLD HOUSES COULD PROVIDE. SO, WHEN GLASS BECAME CHEAPER AND MORE WIDELY AVAILABLE IN THE 19TH CENTURY, PLANTS WERE ABLE TO COME INDOORS.

THE FIRST INDOOR PLANTS WERE GROWN ON A LARGE SCALE BY THE WEALTHY IN GREENHOUSES IN THE LATE 18TH CENTURY. GARDENERS COMPETED TO SEE WHO COULD GROW THE LARGEST AND MOST EXOTIC BLOOMS, AND HOTHOUSES REACHED A CRESCENDO IN THE LATE 19TH CENTURY. THE FIRST HOUSEPLANTS DID NOT APPEAR IN HUMBLER HOMES UNTIL THE MIDDLE OF THE CENTURY, BUT TODAY WE ARE SPOILED FOR CHOICE AS THERE IS A HUGE RANGE OF INDOOR PLANTS AVAILABLE.

HOUSEPLANTS LIVE IN AN ENTIRELY UNNATURAL ENVIRONMENT AND RELY ON YOU FOR ALL THEIR NEEDS. GIVE THEM THE BEST START BY PROVIDING THEM WITH THE RIGHT GROWING MEDIUM.

Soil & food

IMPORTANT NEEDS

Houseplants have needs similar to those of garden plants: light, water, a fertile growing medium, and a certain temperature. They also need to have adequate ventilation and fertilizer. The right potting soil is particularly important. It must be light and loose for drainage and air, but not so light that nutrients drain away.

Bags of ready-made potting soil are relatively new on the scene; gardeners used to make their own. The most favored base was mole-hill soil – for seed starting and potting soil, mix with a little gravel to give it a loose texture. This is still good practice because the soil is beautifully broken down into fine crumbs, and it is suitable for all but tropical houseplants. However, garden soil is not the ideal potting medium, because it tends to be too dense and may carry insects or diseases – though you can still use it if you sterilize the soil before use (see left).

> **TIP**
>
> A simple way of sterilizing soil at home is to place it in an oven, on a shallow pan or cookie sheet, and bake it at 360°F (180°C) for 45 minutes. But don't try this if you have a sensitive nose – it's a smelly process. Add grit or sand to improve drainage before using as potting soil.

> **MYTH BUSTER**
>
> Some people advise using kitty litter as a substitute for vermiculite and perlite, but don't be tempted to try it. Kitty litter has a clay base and is highly absorbent. It will compact the soil instead of aerating it.

> **TIP**
>
> Houseplants can become heavier than the pots they grow in. Think of a blooming amaryllis (*Amaryllis bella-donna*) on a 2 ft (60 cm) stem, a dracaena (*Cordyline dracaena* spp.) in a tall thin pot, or a large cyclamen (*Cyclamen* spp.). Add ½ inch or 1 cm of sand to the top of the pot to stop top-heavy plants tipping over.

CYCLAMEN

POTTING SOIL

Soilless mixes based on peat or peat substitute and other materials are best for most houseplants. These have the added advantage of being light, so you can move even large house-plants around if you need to. But if you have space to do so, make your own houseplant potting soil.

HOMEMADE POTTING SOIL

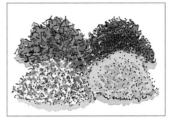

Step 1
Using a 1 qt (1 L) flower pot as a measure, combine 1 pot commercial topsoil, 1 pot peat or coir, 1 pot perlite or builders' sand, plus 1 pot vermiculite for a lightweight mix.

Step 2
Add 1 tablespoon bone meal and a handful of dried manure to provide essential nutrients.

Step 3
Mix thoroughly and leave to stand for 24 hours before using. Store in a covered container for up to a year.

FEEDING

Indoor plants are living in an entirely artificial environment and need regular feeding. You can buy soluble granular, stick, or timed-release fertilizers, or water your plants with garden tea once a month (see page 69).

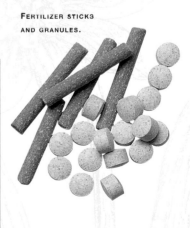

FERTILIZER STICKS AND GRANULES.

AMARYLLIS

MORE HOUSEPLANTS DIE FROM TOO MUCH OR TOO LITTLE WATER THAN FROM ANY OTHER CAUSE. SO LEARN HOW TO GIVE YOUR PLANTS THE MOISTURE THEY NEED.

Watering

CHOOSE THE RIGHT POT

One of the most common causes of plant failure is overwatering, causing root rot. Overwatering means certain death. Underwatered plants wilt and collapse but can usually be revived. When you're starting out, choose terracotta pots. They are porous and lose up to half the water you give them directly through their walls, so you are not likely to overwater. Plastic or glazed pots lose no water through their walls, so plants dry out more slowly.

TIP

• If houseplants are in a variety of containers, don't water them all at the same time, as clay, plastic, and metal pots store and lose water at different rates.

• Give cyclamen *(Cyclamen spp.)* a hot sauna once a month. Place pots on a tray of pebbles and pour boiling water over the pebbles, allowing the steam to rise into the foliage.

Cyclamen don't like wet leaves or crowns, so you should always water them from below.

MYTH BUSTER

Houseplants and greenhouse plants do not like cold water. You should use water at least as warm as the air temperature in the room. Water that is too cold shocks the plant's system; it can damage roots and cause white, scarred leaves.

WHEN TO WATER

Try not to let a plant dry out. Every time a plant wilts, it loses several days of flowering life. Once you've been gardening for a while you can follow the old method of just picking up a pot to see whether a plant needs watering. If it's heavy, all's well; if it's light, it needs water. But the best method for beginners is to stick your index finger into the soil to just above the first joint. If it feels damp, don't water. If it feels dry, water well.

AFRICAN VIOLET

TOP OR BOTTOM?

Most plants can be watered from above, but the leaves of some plants rot when wet. The hairy leaves of plants like African violets (*Saint-paulia* spp.) stain and scorch if any water is splashed onto them, so water them from below. You can immerse plants in a tub of water, or fill saucers of water under the pot. Never leave a plant sitting in water for more than fifteen minutes.

WHAT KIND OF WATER?

Gardeners used to throw cooking water over plants, wash out milk churns onto flowerbeds, and even threw left-over beer into the garden to make sure nutrients weren't wasted. Most people now use tap water on house plants, but it may contain fluoride and chlorine which can build up to harmful levels in the soil. In hard-water areas you may develop salty deposits on pots and the soil surface, but water that's been treated with a water softener is equally bad because it contains other minerals to counterbalance high calcium levels. If you use tap water alone, feed plants with liquid fertilizer to keep a balance of minerals in the potting soil.

VACATION WATERING

If you can't get a neighbor to water for you when you're on vacation, devise a self-watering system for your plants. Line your bathtub with newspaper or old towels to prevent scratching, then place plants on bricks in the tub. Make wicks from several strands of thick yarn and place one or two wicks in each plant pot – more for unglazed clay pots. Fill the tub with water to the top of the bricks and dangle the wicks into the water. If your bathroom is light, plants can last like this for a couple of weeks.

TIP

Vegetable water is perfect for houseplants, because it contains all sorts of nutrients from cooked vegetables. Old aquarium water is also oxygen- and nutrient-rich, and houseplants love it.

To mist or not to mist?

Some plants need high levels of humidity and need to be misted with water regularly.

Houseplants that need high humidity

Aluminum plant (*Pilea cadierei*)
Bird's-nest fern (*Asplenium nidus*)
Corn plant (*Dracaena fragrans*)
Maidenhair fern (*Adiantum raddianum*)
Peacock plant (*Calathea makoyana*)
Flamingo flower (*Anthurium scherzerianum*)
Trailing begonia (*Pellionia daveauana*)
Wandering Jew (*Tradescantia zebrina*)
Zebra plant (*Aphelandra squarrosa*)

SELF-WATERING POT

Step 1
Carefully remove the plant from its pot.

Step 2
Take a small plastic tub a bit larger in diameter than the flower pot, and drill a hole in the lid.

Step 3
Thread a wool or cotton wick through one of the pot's drainage holes.

Step 4
Push the wick into the root ball of the plant, using a pencil or stick.

Step 5
Fill the plastic tub with water, replace the lid, and place the potted plant on top.

MISTER

121

PLANTS ARE LIKE
HUMANS: THEY GET
MISERABLE IF THEY
DON'T GET ENOUGH
LIGHT, AND THEY
STOP FUNCTIONING
PROPERLY WITHOUT
ADEQUATE HEAT.

Light & heat

A PASSION WAS BORN

Perhaps the first houseplant craze was
initiated in Britain when members of
florists' societies – many of whom
worked in northern textile mills and
collected and exhibited plants as a
hobby – introduced auriculas (Primula
auricula) onto their windowsills, and
competed to breed and show the most
impressive hybrids. Auriculas do not
need much direct light, hence their
attraction. You sometimes still see them
shown today in "auricula theaters,"
arrangements of tiered clay pots. This is
how they were originally grown to make
the most of the available light and space,
and to keep air circulating around them.

WHICH LIGHT?

Different plants have varying light requirements,
but there are some rules of thumb. Tropical and
Mediterranean plants need direct sunlight. All
flowering plants, cacti, and succulents need
some direct sunlight. Foliage plants generally
need bright light but not direct sunlight, with
variegated forms requiring more light. Ferns
and evergreen foliage plants need semishade
or filtered light. Wealthy 19th century gardeners
built special fern houses to provide ferns with a
dappled light and humid atmosphere.

Watch out for signs of light deprivation: growth
will be minimal or spindly, variegated leaves
may turn green, blooms will be poor (if any),
and lower leaves will fall or yellow. If plants
have too much light, the leaves develop scorch
patches and lower leaves will wilt by midday.

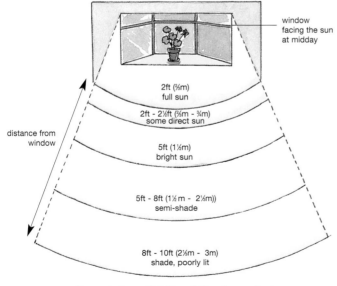

**If your plants need bright sunlight, make sure they're
placed near a window facing toward the midday sun.**

TEMPERATURE

Houseplants generally don't like extremes of heat and cold, and they like to grow accustomed to their preferred temperature and stay there. If you move plants from room to room they will not thrive, as they need to adjust gradually to changes in temperature as well as light and humidity.

SUMMER SUN

If you have the space and shelter, many houseplants like to live outside during a warm summer, when nighttime temperatures are consistently above 55°F (12°C). But keep light-sensitive plants, such as African violets (*Saintpaulia* spp.), cast-iron plants (*Aspidistra elatior*), and peace lilies (*Spathiphyllum* spp.) indoors.

AURICULAS

Only tropical plants like consistent temperatures over 75°F (25°C). They also need high humidity.

Most common houseplants flourish between 60°F - 75° F (15°C - 25°C). Tender plants will struggle at 60°F (15°C).

Less tender houseplants survive between 50°F - 60°F (10°C - 15°C) during their dormant winter period.

PEACE LILY

IF YOU THINK THAT BUGS WON'T FIND YOUR
PLANTS INDOORS, YOU COULDN'T BE MORE
WRONG. HOUSEPLANTS ARE PRONE TO PESTS
AND DISEASES BECAUSE THEY HAVE FEWER
DEFENSES THAN THEIR OUTDOOR RELATIVES.

Poinsettias were once
thought poisonous, but
they are no longer on
official toxic plant lists.

Pests & problems

KEEP YOUR HOUSEPLANTS BUG-FREE

You can keep pests and disease at bay outdoors with natural
assets, such as beneficial predators and companion planting.
The choices are fewer indoors, but there are still ways to keep
your houseplants bug-free, without resorting to chemicals.

First off, try to keep your plants as stress-free as possible. Give
them the conditions they need, and keep them in the appropriate type and size of pot. Potted plants prefer fairly snug containers. A plant will tell you when it needs repotting by sending
roots out through its drainage holes, wilting easily, and producing small, yellow leaves.

MYTH BUSTER

Some companion planting works indoors.
Grow marigolds *(Tagetes minuta)* in pots on
sunny sills among your other plants, because
their leaf exudations help repel insect pests
and some diseases. Pots of lavender may
also have some effect, and pots of thyme
(Thymus spp.*)* or basil *(Ocimum basilicum)*
on your windowsill should keep most flying
pests away.

Group pots of herbs
together on a sunny
windowsill to help
them grow and to
keep pests away.

CLEAN LEAVES

Check your plant leaves often to keep them from getting clogged with dirt and dust, and for signs of insects. Keep the leaves clean by misting them or washing them thoroughly in lukewarm water. Wash large plants under the shower and wipe the leaves of smaller plants with a soft cloth. If there is an insect problem, use insecticidal soap; apply soapy water, leave it for an hour, then rinse off. You can add a little horticultural oil to the soap to help it to stick to the leaves. This also helps the soap to penetrate a soft-bodied insect's waxy coating.

OLD-FASHIONED REMEDIES

Use the kitchen and garden store recipes listed on pages 110-111 to spray indoor plants just as you would outdoor ones, or use the insect-control methods suggested on pages 92-93. All are non-toxic.

The best way to clean large plants is to give them a gentle, cool shower.

TO ENSURE THAT YOUR
FLOWERS LAST AS LONG
AS POSSIBLE, FOLLOW
TIPS HANDED DOWN FROM
COUNTRY PEOPLE FOR
MANY GENERATIONS.

Flower arranging

BEST FLOWER COLLECTING TIME

It is age-old advice to collect flowers early on dry mornings, so they do not wilt too soon. Plants are at their peak then, fresh and unstressed. Most scented flowers including lilies, roses, and sweet peas, are best picked when the dew is still on them, otherwise pick flowers as the dew is just evaporating. Flowers picked in damp weather are likely to rot quickly.

> ### TIP
>
> Flower arrangements last longer if they include foxgloves *(Digitalis* spp.*)*. Or add a cup of foxglove tea made by steeping the leaves or flowers in boiling water for two hours. A cupful of horsetail tea in a vase also helps, as it contains minerals that cut flowers can absorb.

LET THEM REST

Old cottages and farmhouses had cool, dark pantries where cut flowers were left in buckets for a few hours before arranging them. Get into the habit of placing flowers in a cool, shady place in a bucket of lukewarm water before arranging. Wrap the stalks of tulips *(Tulipa* spp.*)* in newspaper as soon as they are cut, before putting them in the bucket. Asters *(Aster* spp.*)* and delphiniums *(Delphinium* spp.*)* thrive if you add a tsp of sugar to each pt (½ L) of water. Change cut flowers' water at least every other day to help them last.

○ **Wrap tulip stems to staunch loss of sap, before putting them in water.**

> ### MYTH BUSTER
>
> It is not just an old wives' tale but good practice to place a small piece of charcoal in every vase of cut flowers. Charcoal attracts bacteria and keeps the water fresh and odor-free.

LILIES AND LEAVES

Combine flowers and leaves to make a striking arrangement.

TIP

• Most flowers last longer in water if their stems are snipped and squashed, but some flowers have different preferences. Flowers with hard stems, such as honeysuckle (*Lonicera* spp.) and lilac (*Syringa* spp.), keep longer if the stem ends are split. Cut off a tiny bit more every couple of days when you change the water so that the stems don't rot.

• Immerse the cut ends of chrysanthemums (*Chrysanthemum* spp.) and azaleas (*Azalea* spp.) in boiling water for a minute before placing them in cold water for a couple of hours. Or singe the ends of azalea stems over a flame just after they've been cut. Lilies (*Lilium* spp.) last longer if you turn them upside down and run cold water over the stems for about a minute before arranging.

SPRING FLOWER ARRANGEMENT

Step 1
Scrunch up chicken wire and make a base for the arrangement. Top up with water. Use foliage to form the shape of the arrangement, and start adding your flowers, one by one.

Step 2
Choose long-lasting flowers as the mainstay of your arrangement. With the leaves, they will give it structure.

Step 3
Add some complementary flowers – they don't need to be as long lasting, as you can replace them, continually rebooosting your arrangement.

TIP

• If cut flowers go limp soon after arranging, you can revive them the old-fashioned way by adding a sprig of willow or meadowsweet to the vase. The modern equivalent is to add half an aspirin to the water.

• Queen Anne's lace (*Anthriscum sylvestris*) looks beautiful as a cut flower. Gather the whole plant, with its root, just before it comes into bloom, and it will last for over a week indoors.

CHAPTER 7

GARDENER'S WELL-BEING

"THE KISS OF THE SUN FOR PARDON, THE SONG OF THE BIRDS FOR MIRTH. ONE IS NEARER GOD'S HEART IN A GARDEN THAN ANYWHERE ELSE ON EARTH."

GARDENING CAN ALSO BE HARD WORK, YET YOU NEVER SEE AN OLD-FASHIONED GARDENER IN A HURRY. FOLLOW THEIR EXAMPLE AND MAKE THINGS EASY FOR YOURSELF: PLAN YOUR GARDEN REALISTICALLY; DECIDE HOW MUCH YOU CAN DO; GROW PLANTS IN THE RIGHT CONDITIONS; PLACE TOOLS, COMPOST, AND WATER NEARBY; AND TAKE CARE.

HERBAL REMEDIES HAVE BEEN USED THROUGHOUT HISTORY. GROW YOUR OWN MEDICINE CHEST AND FIRST AID KIT, AND PRODUCE YOUR OWN COSMETICS AND HOUSEHOLD CLEANSERS. DO NOT TRY TO TREAT SERIOUS OR LONG-TERM MEDICAL PROBLEMS WITHOUT FIRST CONSULTING YOUR PHYSICIAN.

TAKE TIME TO PLAN YOUR GARDEN BEFORE YOU PICK UP A SPADE. HELP YOUR GARDEN TO HELP YOU AND REMEMBER THAT YOUR GARDEN SHOULD BE A PLEASURE, NOT A CHORE.

Lessen the strain

FLOWERING DOGWOOD

MYTH BUSTER

Seeds do not have to be sown exactly when it says so on the packet! Don't watch the clock but the weather. If the ground is too cold and wet, seeds will not have a chance. Remember the old adage to sow dry and plant wet, and wait for a spell of sunny dry weather. Your seedlings will catch up.

TROWEL IN SOIL

PLANNING YOUR GARDEN

Early country gardeners had little opportunity to choose from a wide range of plants. They brought useful and pretty plants in from the wild, and accepted gifts from neighbors and fellow gardeners. But you can spend valuable time in winter planning your garden. Even if your garden is tiny you can always grow a few herbs and vegetables; produce fresh from your garden is without equal. Also include some plants for scent and some for herbal pick-me-ups, potions, and lotions.

As soon as the first bright days of spring arrive it can be very tempting to rush out into the garden and plunge into heavy work. But resist the temptation; nature is not in too much of a hurry in spring, and you shouldn't be either. Old wisdom was to sow beans as the first crop on February 2: "Sow the first in the year when Candlemas is here" but then to wait to plant other crops until "after the dogwood winter," the usual period of cold weather following the blossoming of dogwood (*Cornus spp.*) in spring.

CLOTHING

You don't need special coveralls, but a sturdy pair of boots for comfort and protection, and some warm outerwear are good basics. A common saying is that a gardener needs "a cast-iron back with a hinge in it," because gardening involves bending, stooping, pushing, and carrying. Keeping your back warm is the best way to help prevent "gardener's back." If aches and pains creep in, then use a home remedy from "gardener's first aid" on pages 152-155.

GARDENING GLOVES

One of the joys of making a garden is to create an outdoor space where you can relax. Too many gardeners seem to overlook this. Gardens are not made in a moment; the best ones take years. Remember this, and take time to enjoy the good bits. If you live a hectic lifestyle, you will really reap the benefits if you spend a few moments of peace in your garden just as the sun rises and the dew is evaporating. That's when your herbs and flowers smell strongest because the essential oils begin to evaporate in the warmth, the first flush of insects are getting to work, and birds are active. It will remind you that your garden is a pleasure, and the hard work is worthwhile.

 The right equipment makes gardening safer, easier, and much more satisfying.

MYTH BUSTER

• "You can't race the seasons" is old but good advice. Unless you have a greenhouse, don't let anyone tell you there is any advantage to sowing and planting early. Late frosts kill young plants and they take longer to get going in cold soil. Seeds sown too early indoors turn into straggly, weak-rooted seedlings as they wait to be planted out into soil that is warm enough for them, but if you sow late your plants will catch up. So take things slowly, but don't let them get out of hand.

• Don't start too many jobs at once. There is nothing more disheartening than beginning several big projects and failing to finish them when other seasonal tasks require your attention. Few of us can spend as much time as we might like in the garden, so decide what your priorities are, and stick to them.

YOU DON'T NEED MANY TOOLS, BUT THEY
CAN MAKE ALL THE DIFFERENCE BETWEEN
COMFORTABLE, PLEASURABLE GARDENING
AND MISERABLE HARD WORK.

Tools

LOW BUDGET TOOLS

"Neither wise nor fools can work without tools."
Today garden tools of all descriptions are
widely available, so start with a good spade
and fork, and progress from there later. There is
an old saying that "tools, like boots, are dear if
they are cheap." It is much better to have a few
good tools than a heap of shoddy ones. Start
off with the best basic tools you can afford, and
leave the rest until you know what you want.

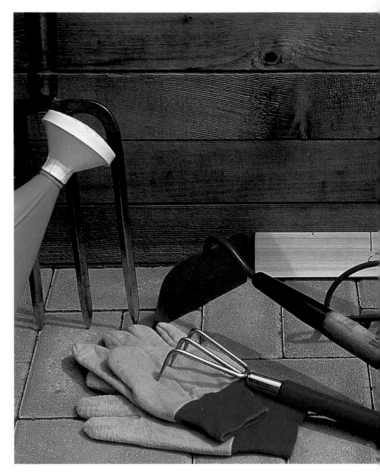

> **TIP**
>
> The handles on good tools
> wear out much faster than
> the tools themselves.
> Increase the life of wooden
> handles by wiping them
> with linseed oil twice a year,
> and never leave them out in
> the rain.

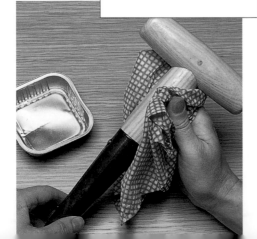

MAKE YOUR OWN TOOLS

A resourceful gardener can create numerous safe, comfortable
– and cheap – gadgets. Make a rake by hammering galvanized
nails into a strip of wood. A broken broom handle serves the
same purpose as a dibble in planting seedlings. Mark lines on
it to check how deep a hole you're making. A hoe is useful, but
a piece of slate or an old blade bound to a broom handle or
length of pipe works just as well until you can buy one. If you
don't like bending over to weed, get a long-handled hand fork
and trowel or convert your own with a piece of pipe.

○ Choose your tools carefully. Begin with the basics and gradually increase your collection. Buy the best you can afford – or improvise.

TIP

• Don't waste time looking for things – hand tools are easy to lose among foliage, so tie colored twine to the handles and make a belt to clip them to.

• Don't store a garden mower over winter on a concrete floor – it can get damp and rust. Instead, raise it off the ground slightly on some slats of wood.

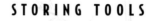

STORING TOOLS

Tools should always be cleaned thoroughly after use so they last longer, and so you don't unwittingly spread disease. The easiest way to spread soilborne diseases is by digging with a dirty spade and fork. Sharpen your spade every season and keep it clean so that it cuts through soil or turf easily.

The best way to clean steel tools is in a sandbox. Find a box deep enough to hold the blade of your spade. Fill it with sand and a bit of mineral oil. Every time you come in from working, plunge the blade of your tool into the sandbox to clean and oil it. The sandbox will last for several years without needing to be refilled, and your tools should last for decades.

MYTH BUSTER

"For if in your house a man shoulders a spade, for you and your kinsfolk a grave is half made." The traditional rhyme expresses the old belief that garden tools should never be carried indoors by the gardener or the sharp edge of the tool would cut down the fortunes of the family. To lay a rake on the soil with its teeth pointing upward was also considered to bring bad fortune. African-American field hands in the Southern United States believed that it was unlucky to leave a hoe standing upright outside overnight. All are based on good practice.

○ Before storing your spade, knock off any dirt and clean the blade in a box of sand.

Sunshine & pollen

REMEDIES FOR HAY FEVER

THERE IS NOTHING MORE PLEASANT THAN WORKING OUTSIDE IN THE GARDEN ON A WARM SUNNY DAY. BUT WATCH OUT FOR TOO MUCH SUN OR PROBLEMS WITH POLLEN.

Hay fever can make working outside in the garden a real misery. Airborne pollens irritate sufferers' mucous membranes, and they experience runny noses and eyes, and may suffer constant sneezing. Spring hay fever comes from the pollen of trees such as oak *(Querus spp.)* and elm *(Ulmus* spp.*)*; the summer type, from the pollen of plants such as grasses and plantain *(Plantago major)*; and fall hay fever is due principally to the pollen of ragweed *(Ambrosia artemisifolia)*.

An old remedy for hay fever assumes that pollen collected by the honey bee will be digested and deposited into the honey it makes. If a sufferer eats minute amounts of this honey, in honeycomb form, they will gradually become immune to the allergy and irritation of these pollens.

↪ **The traditional gypsy remedy for hay fever is to pick fresh mint *(Mentha spp.)* every day, put it in a muslin bag, and sleep with it by your pillow. In two or three weeks, symptoms disappear. Herbalists prescribe mint against many upper respiratory diseases.**

MYTH BUSTER

Goldenrod *(Solidago spp.)* has been blamed by many people as a chief cause of hay fever. Since hay fever is caused by airborne pollen, goldenrod cannot be the culprit because it is pollinated by insects rather than by the wind. This mistaken belief may be because goldenrod blooms at the same time as the real perpetrator, ragweed *(Ambrosia artemisifolia)*, a member of the same family.

GOLDENROD

MYTH BUSTER

Lemons were used for centuries to keep skin pale. Because they are acidic, they were seen to act as bleach, even to the skin. However, because citrus fruits contain coumarins that are phototoxic, using them on your skin before you go into the sun could cause sunburn.

SUNSHINE

Since ancient times people have sought sun therapy. To the Egyptians, sunbathing was quite literally therapeutic, as they bathed in special shallow pools in the sunshine.

Nowadays we are all aware of the dangers of overexposure to sun and fears of skin cancer through too much exposure to radiation. But the tables may have turned too far. We all need sun and it is good for us, as long as we're sensible. Old-fashioned gardeners would never be seen without a hat and long sleeves; follow their example and stay out of the midday sun.

MYTH BUSTER

• If you do catch too much sun, plenty of traditional plant remedies have been passed down over centuries. An ancient Greek pain reliever for sunburn is soothing, sweet-smelling rose petals steeped in astringent vinegar. Russian peasants used potatoes for nearly everything, and grated a potato in oil as a sunburn lotion – the B-complex vitamins in potatoes are very good for the skin.

• An easy, effective sunburn reliever is a compress of fresh cucumber juice – collect the juice by placing thin slices of peeled cucumber in a bowl for two hours and filtering it through a fine cloth. Or apply the soothing juice of the aloe vera (Aloe vera) plant to the affected parts. The flowers and leaves of the humble chickweed (Stella media), steeped in boiling water, then cooled, make a soothing solution for hot and inflamed skin.

The best way to avoid sunburn is to take sensible precautions. Wear a hat and cover your arms when working in summer heat.

PLANTS HAVE THEIR OWN WAYS OF ATTRACTING AND REPELLING INSECTS IN THE GARDEN. FOLLOW THEIR EXAMPLE AND YOU WON'T BE BOTHERED BY GNATS, MOSQUITOES, AND OTHER BITING INSECTS.

Insect repellents

Try wearing a garland of walnut leaves to keep flies away when you're gardening.

PLANTS THAT KEEP INSECTS AWAY

The plant world offers a range of natural insect repellents. When you're gardening, try wearing a garland of walnut leaves *(Juglans regia)* to keep flies away. Pots of growing herbs, such as thyme *(Thymus* spp.*)* and basil *(Ocimum basilicum),* on windowsills may keep flying insects away from the house. In Spain the sticky roots of elecampane *(Inula helenium)* are hung inside the windows as fly traps.

CATNIP

JOE-PYE WEED

Grow pots of pungent herbs, such as thyme, near an outdoor seating area to discourage biting insects.

TIP

• If ants are a pest, keep them from the house by scattering catnip *(Nepeta cataria)* flowers on window-sills, and other entry points.

• To destroy wasps' nests, Native Americans used to smoke them out by burning Joe-pye weed *(Eupatorium purpureum).* Since Joe-pye weed is considered unsafe for oral consumption, this practice is no longer recommended.

MYTH BUSTER

Throughout much of France walnut trees were traditionally valued as highly as an acre of land. Their virtues were not only their wood and their nuts, but because walnut trees "made fat cows and horses." Insects dislike the aroma of walnut leaves so animals could rest peacefully in their shade.

• The best defense against mosquitoes is the bat. A single bat can find and eat over 500 mosquitoes an hour, so build or buy a bat house and encourage bats into your yard.

• A sliced onion pressed onto an insect bite relieves irritation and prevents swelling. This is because onions have cooling and antiseptic properties.

MYTH BUSTER

Nature often places a plant antidote near an irritant – like dock *(Rumex* spp.*)* growing near nettles *(Urtica* spp.*)* to relieve nettle stings. Citronella grass *(Cymbopogon nardus)* is native to the malarial area of Sri Lanka where disease-carrying mosquitoes breed. This lemon-scented grass has a pungent perfume and its principal chemical constituents – geraniol and citronellol – are powerful antiseptics. However, the oil of the stoneroot *(Collinsonia canadensis)* is also sold as citronella, and this does not work as an insect repellent.

BITES AND STINGS

If you get bitten by mosquitoes or wasps, soothe the stings with astringent lemon juice or apple cider vinegar. Bees leave their barbed stings behind and these must be removed.

Step 1
Remove the sting with tweezers, holding the sting near the skin and being careful to avoid gripping the poison sac.

poison sac

Step 2
Then wash the area with baking soda.

Step 3
Rub lavender stems or flowers onto the affected area to remove the discomfort of a bee or wasp sting. Never use lavender oil straight on your skin, as it is too powerful an irritant.

Nettle juice is another good instant sting remedy, and astringent witch hazel *(Hamamelis virginiana)* should be a medicine cupboard staple even if it is not growing in your garden.

EATING OUTDOORS

Eating outside in the evening is less of a pleasure if you also become a meal for the mosquitoes. For complete protection, you're better off staying indoors at dusk when mosquitoes are on the hunt, as no plant is strong enough to repel them for long.

If you know you aren't prone to rashes, stave off biting insects by rubbing a handful of fresh elder *(Sambucus nigra)* leaves or lavender *(Lavendula* spp.*)* stems on your arms, legs, and neck. This is effective for about 20 minutes, then you'll need to rub more on. Chamomile *(Matricaria chamomilla)* or wormwood *(Artemisia absinthium)* will do as well. Citronella is one of the most effective deterrents, so consider lighting citronella candles.

PLANTS HAVE ALWAYS BEEN CREDITED WITH POWERS TO HELP HUMANS. THE EARLIEST GARDENERS GREW PLANTS NOT FOR DECORATION OR EVEN FOR FOOD, BUT BECAUSE OF BELIEF IN THEIR MAGICAL AND HEALING POWERS.

Positive plants

ANTI-WITCH PLANTS

No early country garden was complete without plants to keep witches and evil spirits away. They included the bay tree *(Laurus nobilis)* "the plant of the good angels," hawthorn *(Craetagus* spp.*)*, St.-John's-wort *(Hypericum perforatum)*, and rowan *(Sorbus aucuparia)*. English country gardeners used to spike their seedbeds with rowan and birch *(Betula* spp.*)* twigs on dangerous May mornings when fairies were about.

POT MARIGOLD

Many old cottages have doorways framed in honeysuckle. It was believed to bring good luck, and also kept odors out.

MYTH BUSTER

Lightning plants were believed to protect the home from storms. They included houseleek *(Sempervivum* spp.*)* and stonecrop *(Sedum spectabile)*. This was probably based on sympathetic magic: the plants grew on roofs, and their leaves were deeply serrated, rather like jagged lightning flashes.

SYMBOLIC PLANTS

Honeysuckle *(Lonicera* spp.*)* was another powerful anti-witch plant. Planted by the house door, it reputedly kept fevers and bad spirits out, and by the barn it protected the cattle. It was a symbol of womanly love and brought luck to lovers. Mistletoe *(Viscum album)* had similar attributes. It was a symbol of fertility and a potent healer. Some country folk kept a sprig of mistletoe hanging indoors all year believing "while mistletoe stays in the house, love also stays."

Marital harmony was promised by many plants: "On each side let myrtle grow, so the house no strife shall know." Girls used pot marigold *(Calendula officinalis)* and rosemary *(Rosmarinus officinalis)* as love charms. The cuckoopint *(Arum maculatum)* was believed by young men to bring them the pick of attractive girls, because of its phallic shape.

FOXGLOVES OR FAIRIES' FINGERS

Foxgloves *(Digitalis spp.)* have always been considered magical plants, associated with fairies. They were ever-present in country gardens as protection from evil spirits and fairy charms. Belief in their magical powers continued over many centuries. When descending into mines, 19th century German miners carried foxgloves as talismans to ward off evil spirits.

Foxgloves are powerful healing plants, but they are toxic and should not be used in home remedies. The crucial chemicals in the plants were among the first to be scientifically isolated, and digitoxin and digoxin have been used medicinally for almost two hundred years as heart stimulants.

ELDERFLOWER

ELDERFLOWER CORDIAL

Step 1
Pick 2 or 3 good sized heads of elderflower, wash them under gently running water, and place them in a large earthenware jug.

Step 2
Wash 2 large unwaxed lemons, slice them thinly, and add to the jug with 2 lbs (1 kg) of preserving sugar, 2 tbsps of white vinegar, and 1 gal (5 L) of cold water.

Step 3
Cover with a cotton or muslin cloth and leave the jug for 24 hours in a cool, dark place, such as a pantry floor or a shady garden shed.

Step 4
Strain through a fine sieve into screwtop bottles. It will be ready to drink in 10 days and will keep for several months if stored in a cool place. Once opened, store bottles in the refrigerator.

ELDER

Elder *(Sambucus nigra)* is an important plant in folklore and the most widely used plant in North European folk medicine with "the unusual distinction of being useful in every part." Considered sacred and magical for centuries, the magic had a dark side: people believed a witch could change herself into an elder, and burning elder wood was said to "bring the Devil." This may be because elder is too valuable to misuse.

An early admonition against child abuse suggested that whipping children with elder stunted their growth: "A child that's beat with elder withe will fade away and never thrive." However, cornfields beaten with elder sticks were deemed safe from blight. Perhaps the smell of elder kept pests from the crop; their leaves were strewn on the floor of a room or barn to keep fleas away.

Elder was used to tell the seasons, summer lasting from when the elderflowers bloom to when the berries drop. Berries picked on St. John's Day (June 23) were believed to cure baldness; they also protected against witchcraft and gave the gatherer magical powers.

Although known as "the medicine chest of the country people," little research has been done on elder's healing properties, so do consult a physician before self-medicating. Traditionally, poultices of leaves were used against headaches and for wounds and sprains; lotions for skin conditions, and to keep flies away; and infusions against colds, sore throats, fevers, and infectious diseases. Elderberries were used to stave off infections; flowers and bark eased rheumatism and arthritis; and elderflower drinks were used against insomnia and depression.

SOME PLANTS ARE POSITIVE BECAUSE THEY
HAVE SO MANY VARIED USES IN THE HOME,
GARDEN, AND MEDICINE CHEST.

More positive plants

○ Every old-fashioned garden contains at least one apple *(Malus spp.)* tree, for food, drink, health, and prosperity.

APPLES

The apple has been a symbol of fruitfulness, prosperity, and rejuvenation throughout history and across cultures. Carrying apple bark is an ancient fertility talisman, and a good crop of apples has long been said to predict twins for the farmer or his animals. In Britain the ancient custom of wassailing apple trees after the New Year still continues. Toasts are made and wassailing carols sung to wish good health and encouragement to the trees for another year. Traditionally young apple trees were never harvested "lest this discourages the tree too soon." Of course this is sound gardening sense, allowing the tree to put its energies into growth rather than fruit and seed production too early.

MYTH BUSTER

"To eat an apple going to bed will make a doctor beg his bread." Apples have been used through history as healing food for many complaints. Modern research shows they may have anticancer properties.

For an outdoor torch, bind a cattail head firmly to a strong stick, and dip the head in oil or wax. This is the equivalent of the traditional northern European rush light. They last for up to a half-hour.

CATTAIL

Some plants have hundreds of uses. Cattail *(Typha* spp.*)* was thoroughly appreciated by Native Americans. They ate the flower heads like corn, and the shoots in soups or stews. They made cakes of cattail pollen and water, wrapped them in cattail leaves, and baked them in the coals of a fire. The flower stems were used for arrows. The starchy roots were an important survival food, as they are nutritious, often abundant, and are available year round. The root starch was also used as a poultice for burns. The pollen was sprinkled on wounds to stop bleeding, and was commonly used as talcum powder for babies.

CATTAIL

TIP

If you pick pussy willow *(Salix caprea)*, you should leave stems in a vase for as long as possible. When you throw them out, use the willow water to water your seedlings. Willow water contains indolebutyric acid, which is a constituent in commercial rooting compound and promotes strong growth.

TIP

Cattail's fibrous stems and leaves can be used like reeds *(Phragmites* spp.*)* or bulrush *(Scirpus* spp.*)* for thatch, baskets, and mats. They are ideal for rush seats. Gather them as soon as they reach full size, then dry them in an airy place. Before you use them soak them overnight to make them supple; they can be split for fine work.

ABSORBENT DOWN

The fluffy, ripe seed heads of cattails produce a mass of down. This used to be soaked in the juice of healing herbs such as yarrow *(Achillea* spp.*)*, bee balm *(Monarda* spp.*)*, or mint *(Mentha* spp.*)*, and used to dress wounds. Native Americans used it for diapers, and in World War II it was used to stuff sleeping bags. Gather cattails' fluffy ripe seed heads as they begin to disintegrate in late summer, break them up, and dry them thoroughly before use.

PUSSY WILLOW

HUNDREDS OF
COMMON GARDEN
PLANTS HAVE BEEN
USED AS HEALING
HERBS FOR
THOUSANDS OF
YEARS, BUT IT
IS ALWAYS WISE
TO CONSULT A
PHYSICIAN BEFORE
SELF-TREATMENT.

Healing plants

ECHINACEA

Echinacea or purple coneflower (*Echinacea purpurea*) was one of the most important healing herbs used by Native Americans, applied to wounds, burns and bites, taken for headaches, stomach aches, coughs, colds, and infectious diseases. The root was chewed to dull pain, and the root or leaves and flowers were made into a paste to deaden external pain and clear up septic sores. Today, echinacea is the most important immune system stimulant in Western herbal medicine. It is used against infections of all kinds, and is one of the few herbs that helps patients recuperate following a viral infection. It is antibiotic, antifungal, antiinflammatory, antiallergenic, and antiseptic.

DRIED ECHINACEA

ECHINACEA

> **TIP**
>
> Try making a paste by crushing the leaves of cone-flowers (*Echinacea* spp.*)* and apply it to stings or bites. You will feel a numbing effect, rather like mild local anesthetic.

ST.-JOHN'S-WORT

St.-John's-wort (*Hypericum perforatum*) is named from the Greek to "protect from evil spirits." In many country areas of Europe it was considered to have magical powers – bunches of the flowers were hung on doors on St. John's Day (June 23rd) to protect residents from troubles; a sprig of St.-John's-wort in milk was said to keep milk from turning sour; a sprig in a girl's dress or a man's vest would ensure happiness and prosperity. As a remedy, its use seemed almost universal, it is recorded as a cure for coughs and catarrh, a poultice for sprains, for muscle strain and joint inflammation, as a wound healer and a herb to charm away low spirits.

The hypericin in the oil of St.-John's-wort flowers is antidepressant, enhancing the effect of neurotransmitters in the brain. It is also strongly antiviral and anti-bacterial and recent research suggests it may even have a role to play against cancer. It used to be known as a "sun plant" because of its yellow flowers, but use it with caution, as it can cause sun sensitivity in skin.

For centuries, on St. John's Day (June 23rd), it was traditional to hang St.-John's-wort on the front door as a talisman.

GARLIC

No garden should be without garlic (*Allium sativum*) for the health of gardener and garden. Garlic has always been credited with magical powers as well as being a potent medicine. It was recorded as long ago as 1500 BC as a constitutional strengthener and antidote to poisoning, and has been used continuously as a virtual cure-all.

Before the development of antibiotics, garlic was used to treat infections from tuberculosis to typhoid. It was thought to be an ideal home medicine: the allicin in the bulbs is antiseptic and antibiotic and garlic is also powerfully antibacterial, antiviral, antifungal, and antiparasitic. However, garlic is no use whatever if cooked, and has to be raw to work at all.

MYTH BUSTER

For centuries, people have placed a bowl of sliced onions under a sick person's bed, crediting it with the power to attract the disease out of the patient's body. Onion vapors do help to cure inflammatory wounds and generally act against bacteria, although they should not replace medical treatment.

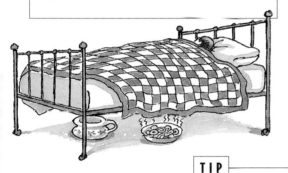

TIP

• Chew peppermint *(Mentha piperita)*, or parsley *(Allium sativum)* to kill the odors of garlic on the breath.

• Black cohosh was also known as bugwort and bugbane because its smell was reputed to deter insects. Try planting it near your outdoor sitting area to keep flies away.

Healing herbs such as basil and mint are delicious eaten in a salad. Other salad herbs include chervil, parsley, and tarragon (see page 147).

BLACK COHOSH

BLACK COHOSH

Black cohosh (*Cimicifuga racemosa*) is a very old remedy of Native Americans. It was known as "squaw root" because infusions of the dried root helped childbirth and with women's problems. It was also used for treating neuralgia. We now know the chemical anemonin in the plant depresses the nervous system and relieves pain, and that salicylates in the plant are antiinflammatories.

NATURE PROVIDES
HUNDREDS OF SIMPLE
REMEDIES. INCLUDE
SOME IN YOUR OWN
GARDEN FOR A
HOME-GROWN
MEDICINE CHEST.

More healing plants

YARROW

Yarrow *(Achillea millefolium)* is an ancient flower, named for Achilles, who used it to staunch the wounds of his soldiers on the battlefield. Yarrow is found to contain the astringent tannin and salicylic acid, which is antiseptic. It is also antiinflammatory. Yarrow belongs to the allergenic Compositae/Asteraceae family, so should be avoided by people allergic to ragweed and goldenrod.

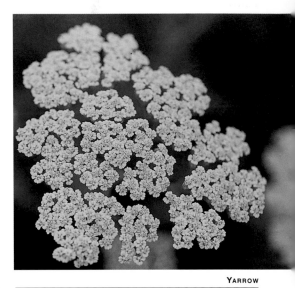

YARROW

> **TIP**
>
> • Yarrow is most potent as a medicine if it is picked when in flower. If you use the plant fresh, make sure it is perfectly clean before putting it on a wound, otherwise you risk introducing harmful organisms and possible infection.
>
> • Just sitting by a bush of lavender *(Lavandula* spp.*)* on a sunny day is a calming and healing experience. The volatile oils, released in the warm sun, have a relaxing effect.

MINT

No garden should be without mint *(Mentha* spp.*)* for food, drink, and health. Commonly drunk to aid digestion, many qualities are ascribed to this rampant herb. It has been said to repel mice and insects, to keep bees at home when rubbed over a beehive, to keep milk from turning sour, and to have aphrodisiac qualities. Mint soaked in vinegar was a traditional remedy for toothache. The oils in mint are antiseptic, antiviral, and antifungal.

POT MARIGOLD

The common pot marigold *(Calendula officinalis)* is a familiar cottage garden flower. In folklore, it was widely considered a magic plant providing the gift of clear sight; a 12th century herbal recommended simply looking at the plant to improve eyesight, clear the head, and encourage cheerfulness. It was also seen as a love charm. On a more practical level, it has antiseptic, antiviral, and bactericidal properties. Calendula ointment heals gardeners' chapped and cracked hands (see page 149).

LAVENDER

FEVERFEW

Feverfew *(Tanacetum parthenium)* is a useful flower, used medicinally by country people for hundreds of years against "aches of the head, aches of the ears, and biting insects," as well as for gynecological complaints. It should not be taken, however, if you are pregnant, breastfeeding, or prone to rashes, and, as it belongs to the allergenic Compositae/Asteraceae family, a physician should be consulted before self-medication.

If you suffer from migraines, chewing three to four dried leaves of feverfew every day may alleviate pain. Chemicals in the leaves inhibit the release of too much serotonin, which is thought to trigger migraine.

FEVERFEW

MYTH BUSTER

Tea made from the leaves of the gingko tree *(Gingko biloba)* helps stimulate the memory. Gingko was originally prescribed for old-people's problems because of sympathetic medicine – gingko is an ancient tree, therefore it will help the elderly. We now know that the leaves contain active constituents that improve circulation to the brain, so more oxygen is delivered and brain function improves. It is thought that gingko could be helpful for Alzheimers' sufferers and may reduce the likelihood of strokes. As it is also a blood thinner, it should not be used without a physician's supervision.

Lemon balm *(Melissa officinalis)* has been commended since the 15th century to "glue together greene wounds," as the hydrocarbons in the oils in lemon balm starve germs of oxygen.

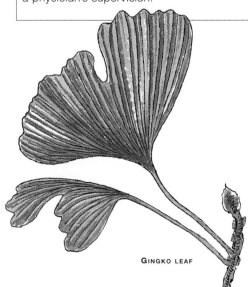

GINGKO LEAF

NETTLES

Don't uproot all the nettles in your garden. "If they'd eat nettles in March and mugwort in May, so many young maidens wouldn't go to the clay." Nettles *(Urtica* spp.*)* are highly nutritious, rich in vitamins A and C and in minerals. They have also been credited with many healing actions. Urtication, or beating yourself with nettles, is an old Russian cure to encourage blood to rise to the surface to improve circulation, and it was also used by the Romans to stave off rheumatism in Britain's cold damp climate. However, you may prefer to use the powerful nettle in teas for coughs, colds, and lung infections, and apply its juice topically for stings, bites, rashes, and nosebleeds.

ORNAMENTAL FLOWERS WERE ORIGINALLY ONLY INCLUDED
IN OLD COUNTRY GARDENS IF THEY HAD SOME USE.
TRADITIONALLY HERBS FOR HEALING AND HERBS FOR
FOOD CAME FIRST. OFTEN THESE TWO ROLES OVERLAPPED.

Kitchen herbs

WILD PLANTS

Every vegetable we grow was once a wild plant, and some
useful food plants still remain outside the garden. Dandelion
leaves are vitamin rich. Blackberries are full of fiber. Rosehips are high
in vitamin C. Some of the earliest plants to be invited into the garden were the
herbs that have been used in kitchens worldwide for thousands of years.

ROSEMARY

Rosemary *(Rosmarinus officinalis)* is an excellent flavoring with most meat
and vegetables, and in drinks. Many country people still believe that if you plant
rosemary bushes in your garden you will never be short of friends. Folklore also
suggests that rosemary will only grow where the woman is boss in the marriage.
It is a magical and sacred herb and is supposed to have had white flowers
before the Virgin Mary spread the child Christ's clothes on a rosemary bush to
dry and its flowers turned blue.

TIP

Dandelion leaves *(Tara-
xacum officinale)* can be
very bitter, but they are
good to eat if picked in
cool weather until the
flowers appear. Use the
young leaves in salads,
or cooked as a pot-herb.
If the leaves are bitter,
change the cooking water
once or twice.

MYTH BUSTER

Compared to traditional vegetables, dandelion leaves are astonishingly nutritious,
containing significant levels of vitamin A,
vitamin C, several B vitamins, and many
minerals including calcium, chlorine, copper,
iron, phosphorus, potassium, magnesium,
silicon, and sulfur.

SAGE

"He that would live for aye should eat sage in May." Sage
(Salvia officinalis) was highly acclaimed as a rejuvenating tonic
for centuries, used in the kitchen and medicine chest. It
stimulates the appetite and
improves digestion, so sage
stuffing has always accompanied
very rich meat to stave off
colic and indigestion. It was
also seen to foretell
prosperity: "As the sage
bush flourishes, so does
the family fortune."

SAGE

Grow kitchen herbs as near as possible to your kitchen, so they are convenient to pick.

CHIVES

CHIVES

The easiest to grow of all the onion family, chives (Allium schoenoprasum) help the health of the garden by keeping pests off rose bushes, they are delicious in salads and cheese and egg dishes, and share the healing qualities of the allium family: antiseptic, antibiotic, antiviral. Whooping cough sufferers apparently needed only eat sandwiches filled with chopped chives for four days and the illness would vanish.

DILL

Grow dill (Anethum graveolens) for its beautiful feathery foliage and as a useful flavoring with fish and in pickles and vinegars. If worried by witches, dill is a useful plant to grow as "Trefoil, vervain, John's-wort and dill, hindereth witches of their will." Early American settlers named dill and fennel seeds "meetinghouse seeds," chewing them to stave off the boredom and hunger of long sessions in church.

Traditional kitchen herbs at a glance

Angelica Leaves in fruit desserts and fish dishes; candy stems and roots.
Basil Mediterranean cooking; with tomatoes; in pesto.
Bay General flavoring for soups, stocks, stews.
Chervil Good in egg dishes, soups, salads.
Chives With cheese and eggs, in potato salad.
Dill With fish; in egg dishes.
Fennel Use seeds in cabbage dishes.
Horseradish In sauces and vinegars; with beef and fish.
Lovage Soups, stocks, stews; with chicken, ham, fish.
Marjoram In savory meat and vegetable dishes.
Mint In savory jellies; with lamb, and in dark chocolate sauce.
Parsley Flavoring for butters and sauces; garnish, salads.
Rosemary With lamb, roast potatoes, fish, herb bread; general flavoring.
Sage With meat dishes; as flavoring with onion.
Savory With beans and brassicas.
Tarragon Salads, eggs, chicken and lamb dishes.
Thyme All savory dishes; with lemons and oranges.

Country herb vinegar

17.5 fl oz (500 ml) white wine vinegar
4 large sprigs of mint, tarragon, basil, thyme, fennel, dill, or rosemary; or 4 peeled garlic cloves.
Push two herb sprigs into a bottle of vinegar. Seal the bottle and leave in a sunny place for 2 weeks. Change the sprigs for fresh ones. Leave for 2 weeks before using.

COUNTRY GARDENERS HAVE ALWAYS USED PLANTS
FROM THEIR GARDENS AS EFFECTIVE HOME CURES.
FOLLOW THEIR EXAMPLE TO MAKE SIMPLE REMEDIES
WITH EVERYDAY INGREDIENTS AND EQUIPMENT.

PREPARING HERBS IN OIL

Step 1
Pack a large jar full of herbs.

Step 2
Fill to the brim with organic sunflower oil. Cover.

Step 3
After 5 days, strain into a bowl through muslin or a jelly bag.

Step 4
Squeeze the herb-filled muslin between your hands, then discard the herbs.

Step 5
Repack the jar with herbs and fill with the strained oil. Repeat the process twice more, then pour the strained oil into bottles. Seal, and store in a cool, dark place.

| TIP |

Soak cotton or muslin in a hot decoction or infusion to make poultices and compresses. A hot water bottle on the poultice helps to keep it warm longer.

Preparing herbs & flowers

GATHERING HERBS AND FLOWERS

Gather herbs and flowers in dry weather first thing in the morning before their essential oils evaporate in the sun. If you are harvesting for storing, spread the plants to dry in a well-ventilated place. Use muslin- or mesh-covered drying frames (see pages 84-5) for flower heads, or hang dry bunches of herbs upside down to dry so that the volatile oils flow into the leaves. Store dried plant material in airtight jars away from direct light and it should be good for several months. Caution: many herbs are unsuitable for making infusions and teas – consult a professional before using.

INFUSIONS AND TEAS

The simplest herbal preparations are made from the leaves or petals of plants. Never boil the herbs. For tea, pour 1 pt (550 ml) of boiling water over fresh herbs (according to the recipe) and leave them to steep for 10 minutes before straining and using. For infusions and washes, use three times the quantities of herbs and steep for 30 minutes.

DECOCTIONS

These are made from bark and roots. Measure according to the recipe, grind the ingredients into a pan, add water, bring to a boil, and simmer, covered, for 10 minutes. Strain while still hot.

DRIED FLOWERS

SYRUP

Add 1 lb (500 g)
honey or 12 oz (360 g) sugar
to 1 pt (550 ml) of an infusion
or decoction and heat until all
the sweetener dissolves. Then cool,
bottle, and store in the refrigerator.

HERBS OR FLOWERS IN OIL

Oil-based infusions or rubbing oils use the same proportions of
liquid to herb as teas or infusions. Before imported oils, country
folk traditionally used pigs' lard, because it was available. But
today use organic sunflower oil. Put the oil and the herb in a
glass bowl over a double boiler and heat gently for about three
hours before straining and storing the oil in sealed bottles in a
cool, dark place.

MAKING OINTMENT

Ointments and creams use herbs macerated in oil with wax added
to make a creamy spreading consistency. Native Americans used to
make creams by cooking plants in fat. Any fat will do, but today it is
easiest to use cold-pressed olive oil.

Step 1
Put 1 pt (550 ml)
of olive oil and 2 oz
(50 g) of wax in a
heatproof dish.

Step 2
Add fresh herbs
– enough to be
completely covered
by the oil mixture.

Step 3
Heat over a double
boiler for a few hours,
then strain the herb
mixture through a
muslin bag.

Step 4
Pour into jars and seal.
The mixture will solidify
quite quickly. Store in
a cool place. Once
opened store in the
refrigerator.

TIP

Always use beeswax in
creams and ointments rather
than synthetic paraffin wax.
Beeswax draws out more of
the herb because it dis-
solves more slowly, and
makes a smoother, better-
scented and more concen-
trated cream.

Beeswax is a good
base for creams and
ointments. You can
mix it with any herb
or flower, and it is a
natural alternative to
synthetic paraffin wax.

MYTH BUSTER

Aromatherapy – using
perfumed essential oils distilled
from plants with massage for
general health – is comparatively
modern, but it builds on ancient
traditions. Perfume has always been
important for country dwellers as much as
for those living in palaces. Country cottages
had fragrant plants outside the door, or around
the window. Most of the plants deemed
suitable to plant at the door for protection also
had beautiful scents – honeysuckle (*Lonicera*
spp.), lilac (*Syringa* spp.), myrtle (*Myrtus*
officinalis), and rosemary (*Rosmarinus*
officinalis). This was necessary to mask the
odors of daily life, and also to lift the spirits.

ROSEMARY

GARDEN TEAS & SYRUPS FOR COMMON AILMENTS

IF YOU'RE FEELING A BIT UNDER THE WEATHER, FOLLOW THE TRADITIONAL PRACTICE OF PICKING COMMON FLOWERS FROM YOUR GARDEN AND HEDGEROW TO MAKE SIMPLE AND EFFECTIVE TEAS AND SYRUPS.

Garden syrups for coughs and colds

Horehound (*Marrubium vulgare*)
Blue vervain (*Verbena hastata*)
Hyssop (*Hyssopus officinalis*)
Wild bergamot (*Monarda fistulosa*)
European elderberry
(*Sambucus nigra*)
Thyme (*Thymus vulgaris*)
for dry coughs

Many traditional cough and cold syrups come from Native Americans, including syrup from horehound (*Marrubium vulgare*) and from the bark of the white pine (*Pinus strobus*). They also commonly held sweat lodges for general detoxification and purification, where sacred and healing herbs such as red cedar (*Juniperus virginiana*) mingled with the smoke. Northern European cultures have long used saunas for general cure-alls – pine branches (*Pinus* spp.) can be thrown onto the coals to help respiratory problems.

BEEBALM

Teas for coughs, colds and flu

Hyssop (*Hyssopus officinalis*)
European elderflower
(*Sambucus nigra*)
Yarrow (*Achillea millefolium*)
Catmint (*Nepeta cataria*)
Lime/linden (*Tilia europaea*)
Thyme (*Thymus vulgaris*)

Elderfire water is a 19th century Irish remedy made by steeping 1 lb (500 g) of ripe elderberries with 4 oz (120 g) of sugar in a bottle of whiskey. Traditionally drunk with hot water before bedtime, it was said "a cold would flee before three days were gone."

Some people prefer to make herb tea in a pot and strain it straight into the cup.

Headaches – teas

Rosemary (*Rosmarinus officinalis*)
Vervain (*Verbena officinalis*)
Feverfew (*Tanacetum parthenium*)
Passionflower (*Passiflora incarnata*)
Lavender (*Lavandula angustifolia*)

PASSIONFLOWER

Infections – teas or decoctions

Echinacea (*Echinacea purpurea*) - flowering plant parts
Lavender (*Lavandula angustifolia*)
St.-John's-wort
(*Hypericum perforatum*)
Elderflower (*Sambucus nigra*)

ST.-JOHN'S-WORT

LIME

Teas for tension/stress

Lavender *(Lavandula angustifolia)*
Lemon balm *(Melissa officinalis)*
Lime/linden *(Tilia europaea)*
St.-John's-wort
(Hypericum pertoratum)

Poor circulation – teas or decoctions

Buckwheat
(Fagopyron esculentum)
Cramp bark (or guelder rose)
(Viburnum opulus)
Angelica *(Angelica archangellca)*
Wild geranium
(Geranium maculatum)

ANGELICA

Arthritis/rheumatism – drink floral teas regularly

Sweet violet *(Viola odorata)*
Rosemary *(Rosmarinus officinalis)*
Evening primrose
(Oenothera biennis)
Echinacea
(Echinacea purpurea)

Hay fever and allergies – drink tea twice a day

Stinging nettle *(Urtica dioica)*
European elderflower
(Sambucus nigra)

Teas for indigestion

Peppermint *(Mentha piperata)*
Dill *(Anethurn graveolens)*
Chamomile
(Matricaria chamomilla)
Lemon balm *(Melissa officinalis)*

The simplest herb teas are made by steeping fresh leaves in boiling water.

PUMPKIN BLOSSOM

Tonic teas

Lemon balm *(Melissa officinalis)*
Pumpkin blossom
(Cucurbita moschata)

Pumpkin blossom tea is a traditional energizing tea containing numerous minerals and vitamins.

Early American settlers drank rose tea to settle the stomach and to ward off fevers.

Sleep-well teas

Chamomile *(Matricaria chamomilia)*
Lettuce *(Lactuca sativa)*
Valerian *(Valeriana officinalis)*
Passionflower *(Passiflora incarnata)*

SUITABLE PLANTS EXIST TO EASE NEARLY EVERY AILMENT, AND EVERY GARDENER SHOULD HAVE A SELECTION OF STAPLES IN THE MEDICINE CHEST. THESE OLD-FASHIONED STANDBYS ARE EASY TO MAKE AND USE.

Gardener's first aid

CALENDULA CREAM

Every home medicine chest should contain all-purpose soothing and antiseptic calendula cream for cuts and grazes. It's an excellent salve for chapped and cracked winter hands:

1 pt (550 ml) oil, 2 oz (50 g) beeswax,
1 handful pot marigold petals (Calendula officinalis)

Melt the oil and wax in a bowl over a double boiler, stir in the herbs, and heat for about two hours then pour the mixture quickly into glass storage jars and store in a cool dark place.

COMFREY OINTMENT

Substitute two handfuls of comfrey leaves (Symphytum officinale), finely chopped, for the pot marigold petals in the calendula ointment recipe.

Antiinflammatory comfrey ointment is the best treatment for bruises and bumps, but must not be used on broken skin.

MYTH BUSTER

Comfrey used to be called knitbone – because comfrey poultices were used to heal fractured limbs. Comfrey baths were once popular before marriage to allegedly repair the hymen and restore virginity!

WITCH HAZEL

CHAMOMILE LOTION

This is a childhood standby to soothe itches, but also a wonderful cooler for sunburn, stings, or bites. Either add a few drops of chamomile oil (Matricaria chamomilla) to a strong infusion (see page 148) of witch hazel (Hamamelis virginiana), or make chamomile salve in the same way as calendula cream.

ROSEMARY BARRIER OINTMENT

Few gardeners remember to wear gloves for every gardening activity. To protect your hands use rosemary *(Rosmarinus officinalis)* barrier ointment before and after gardening.

Step 1
Chop four handfuls of fresh rosemary flower shoots.

Step 2
Follow the standard ointment recipe shown on page 149.

Step 3
Reheat the mixture if it solidifies. Then strain it into glass jars, and store out of direct sunlight in a cool place.

TIP

To draw out a stubborn splinter or thorn, make an ointment from leaves of chickweed *(Stellaria media).* If this is not practical, follow an old shepherd's method and squeeze chickweed over the thorn hole, then bind the leaves over it for a few hours.

Bind a sprain with fresh comfrey or elder leaves. If pain continues for more than 4 hours, seek medical advice.

EUCALYPTUS

EUCALYPTUS OINTMENT

If you suffer a sprain, make an ointment from pulverized eucalyptus *(Eucalyptus gunni)* leaves. The oils in eucalpytus have antispasmodic, antirheumatic, and antineuralgic qualities. Or lay elder *(Sambucus nigra)* or comfrey *(Symphytum* spp.) leaves on the affected limb, as long as there is no broken skin.

GARDENER'S NAIL TREATMENT

To toughen or mend damaged nails, use horsetail *(Equisetum arvense).* It contains high levels of silica to strengthen nails.

Step 1
Place two tablespoons of chopped horsetail into a stainless steel saucepan and cover with a cup of boiled water.

Step 2
Leave to infuse for a half-hour, then strain and pour into a suitable-sized bowl.

Step 3
Soak your finger-nails in the solution for 10 minutes.

ACHES AND PAINS CAN STOP THE PLEASURE OF GARDENING, SO KEEP SOME HOMEGROWN REMEDIES AT HAND.

More first aid

BACKACHE

After a hard day's gardening, ease away nagging aches and pains with rosemary. Make an infusion from three handfuls of rosemary (*Rosmarinus officinalis*) flowerstalks in 1 pt (550 ml) of water, and add it to a warm bath. If you then put a sprig under your bed, folklore decrees you will have pleasant dreams!

Or keep a bottle of sweet-smelling rosemary oil and rub it on inflamed or aching joints.

TIP

Rose petals have a soothing and moisturizing quality. Make rose lip balm with the standard cream/ointment recipe on page 149, but use a quarter of the proportions given.

RHEUMATIC MASSAGE OIL

If rheumatism causes problems on damp days, have a relaxing birch massage. This stimulates and purifies the system, helping rheumatic complaints and easing stress and tiredness from overdoing things.

Fill a large glass jar with white birch leaves (*Betula pendula*), and cover with oil. Place on a sunny windowsill and steep for two weeks before straining. Pour the resulting oil over fresh leaves and allow to steep for another two weeks. Strain through clean muslin, bottle, and store in the refrigerator.

ARTHRITIS RUB

Following the same process, make a massage oil with strips of bark from the white willow (*Salix alba*) and use it to relieve the inflammation and pain of arthritis. Rub it onto affected parts every morning and night.

WHITE BIRCH

MASSAGE FOR UPPER BACK

The upper back is susceptible to gardening-related tension, which can be relieved by a soothing massage with oil. Stop if there is severe pain on pressing the back with the fingers.

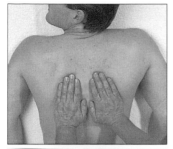

Step 1
Put oiled hands on each side of the spine with the fingers pointing toward the head (don't press on the spine itself). Pressing down, move hands up the back.

Step 2
At the top of the back, continue the movement out toward the shoulders. Cup hands as you massage around the shoulders.

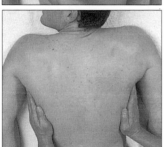

Step 3
Ease off the pressure. Maintain contact with your palm and fingers, and stroke down the outside of the trunk. Repeat the whole process, adding oil to your hands as needed.

RELAXING FOOT BATHS

Soak your feet for 10 minutes in an herbal foot-bath, using a ½ pt (275 ml) strong infusion of lavender *(Lavandula angustifolia)*, lime flowers *(Tilia europeaea)*, rosemary, peppermint *(Mentha piperita)*, thyme *(Thymus vulgaris)*, mugwort *(Artemisia vulgaris)*, or a mixture.

WARMING FOOT BATHS

Add ½ tbsp of chili or cayenne powder to a bowl of hot water to warm and revive chilled feet.

WOUNDS

To cleanse cuts, wash with an infusion of yarrow *(Achillea millefolium)* or pot marigold *(Calendula officinalis)*. Pot marigold will sting but has very good antiseptic qualities.

POOR CIRCULATION AND CRAMP

Peel some bark of the cramp bark *(Viburnum opulus)* in spring and early summer, leaving enough for the tree to stay alive. Dry it and use as a decoction or tea when needed.

COLD SALVE

Native North Americans used a cold salve made from the buds of quaking aspen *(Populus tremuloides)* cooked in fat. An easier remedy is made by steeping eucalyptus leaves *(Eucalyptus gunnii)* in a small jar of vegetable oil, then rubbing a few drops of the oil under your nose or on your chest to ease congestion.

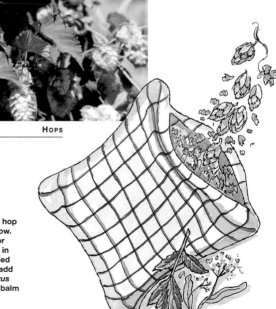

HOPS

Avoid insomnia with a hop *(Humulus lupulus)* pillow. Make a small muslin or cotton bag and place in it three handfuls of dried hop flowers. You can add dried lime lowers *(Citrus aurantifolia)* or lemon balm *(Melissa offcinalis)*.

155

Cosmetics

LADY'S MANTLE

YOUR GARDEN CAN ALSO PROVIDE MANY BASIC INGREDIENTS FOR YOUR BATHROOM CABINET, FROM PREPARATIONS FOR SKIN CARE TO PERSONAL HYGIENE, USING TIMELESS RECIPES MADE FROM HERBS AND FLOWERS.

Garden cosmetics and cleansers care for the body gently. Sometimes plants are used with no preparation – for example, you can rub stalks of cleavers *(Galium aparine)* on your body for a safe deodorant, use sage leaves *(Salvia officinalis)* as an effective tooth cleaner, or use cucumber juice for a skin freshener and toner.

LADY'S CHOICE

Lady's mantle *(Alchemilla vulgaris)* was first recorded as a beauty lotion in the Middle Ages, and was probably used long before that. It's an astrigent and helps to firm the skin. Women believed that their beauty would be enhanced if they used the leaves with beads of morning dew upon them, which was believed powerful enough to turn base metal into gold.

TIP

Dry thyme *(Thymus* spp.*)* leaves and mix with salt for antiseptic toothpowder, or prepare sage in the same way for when fresh leaves are not available. Store in an airtight container.

BORAGE

MYTH BUSTER

A popular 18th century cosmetic for removing freckles was fumitory or fevertory *(Fumaria* spp.*)*. "If you wish to be pure and holy, wash your face with fevertory." It doesn't work, but supposedly it had some use in getting rid of worms – not recommended today!

Herbs and flowers for skin care

Elderflower *(Sambucus nigra)* emollient
Violet *(Viola odorata)* emollient
Marshmallow *(Althaea officinalis)* emollient
Borage *(Borago officinale)* emollient
Comfrey *(Symphytum* spp.*)* emollient
Pot marigold *(Calendula officinalis)* astringent
Tansy *(Tanacetum vulgare)* astringent
Chinese witch hazel *(Hamamelis mollis)* astringent
Horsetail *(Equisetum arvense)* astringent
Lady's mantle *(Alchemilla vulgaris)* astringent
Thyme *(Thymus vulgaris)* toning, refreshing
Yarrow *(Achillea millefolium)* toning, refreshing
Chamomile *(Matricaria chamomilla)* cooling, anti-inflammatory
Lavender *(Lavandula angustifolia)* antiseptic, stimulating

◖ Emollient herbs, such as marshmallow, contain mucilages, compounds that form gels when mixed with water. They soothe and lubricate the skin surface.

SKIN CARE

Buttermilk has been used as the base for a facial cleanser for hundreds of years. If it is hard to find today, you can use full cream milk instead. For the simplest cleanser just wash with an herbal infusion.

One of the advantages of making your own cosmetics is that you can make small quantities and experiment. Match herbal preparations to your skin type. If you have oily skin, use astringent herbs, which tauten the skin. For dry skin, use emollient herbs, which soften, soothe, and lubricate.

HAIR TREATMENTS

Soapwort (*Saponaria officinalis*) has always been used as shampoo and for fine fabrics. It contains saponins, chemicals that foam when added to water. All parts of soapwort produce a gentle cleansing lather.

For shine: rinse with rosemary(*Rosmarinus officinalis*), marigold, sage (*Salvia officinalis*), horsetail, or nettles (*Urtica* spp.).

For blond hair: use chamomile, pot marigold, or yarrow flowers.

For dark hair: use walnut, elder (*Sambucus nigra*) or raspberry leaves, or elderberries.

SOAPWORT SHAMPOO

Use 10 leafy soapwort stems about 8 in (20 cm) long – or 1 oz (30 g) dried soapwort root, and 1 pt (550 ml) water.

Step 1
Cut the soapwort stems or root into short lengths, bruise them slightly with a wooden spoon and place in a stainless steel saucepan.

Step 2
Bring to a boil and simmer for 15 minutes, stirring several times.

Step 3
Cool, strain, and use. Rinse your hair with an herbal infusion.

MYTH BUSTER

Evergreen myrtle *(Myrtus communis)* has long been associated with love, happiness, and long marriage. Myrtle leaves and flowers were used as hair treatments for centuries in the belief they would make hair grow thick, long, and attractive, and to cure baldness. A myrtle rinse does make hair smell pleasant and herbal rinses add a shine, but the other qualities aren't backed up even though they've been recorded since Roman times.

TIP

If you follow the example of the Romans and use elderberries as hair coloring, be careful, as they may also darken your skin.

REDISCOVER SOME
OLD RECIPES FOR
HOME CARE USING
TIPS PRACTICED BY
COUNTRY WIVES IN
PAST CENTURIES.
MANY PLANTS CAN BE
USED IN THE HOUSE
WITH LITTLE OR NO
PREPARATION.

Home care

FURNITURE POLISH

Walnut (*Juglans regia)* and hazelnut (*Coryllus avellana)* kernels make excellent furniture polishes, because oil from the nut is released when you rub the kernel's cut surface over the furniture. Rub first in a circular movement before

WALNUT

working in the direction of the grain. After the oil has dried a little, polish with a soft cloth. Walnuts are particularly effective for darkening pale marks on polished furniture. Make a paste to kill woodworm by crushing horse chestnuts (*Aesculus hippocastanum).* A 17th century furniture polish was made by crushing seeds of sweet cicely (*Myrrhis odorata/Osmorhiza longistylis)* into beeswax.

MYTH BUSTER

• Unassuming plants can be as powerful as any strong chemicals. The leaves of the common wood sorrel (*Oxalis acetosella)* make a natural bleach. To make a strong infusion, steep for an hour or two, and then reboil and use. It works because of the high levels of oxalic acid in the common woodland plant. The juice from its leaves will remove rust spots and ink stains from linen or cotton.

• Moths are rarely a severe problem today, owing largely to improved domestic hygiene. But if you do have a moth problem, natural moth repellents abound. Even if you don't, try leaving sweet woodruff (*Asperula odorata),* meadowsweet (*Filipendula ulmaria),* or worm-wood (*Artemisia abrotanum)* in your clothes and linen; their pleasant scent leaves fabrics smelling fresh. Shavings of cedar wood (*Cedrus spp.)* also do the job.

SWEET CICELY

SCOURING PADS

There's no need to buy scouring pads if you have a supply of horsetail (*Equisetum arvense).* Just scrub with the abrasive, silica-rich stems and leaves. Don't buy expensive marker pens or name tags; stab a pen into a raw sloe (*Prunus spinosa)* and write with the juice on linen and cotton. Early settlers in North America called pokeweed (*Phytolacca americana)* "inkberry" and mashed berries for purplish ink, while their British counter-parts squeezed cornflower (*Centaurea spp.)* petals for blue.

• The French name for southernwood (*Artemisia abrotanum*) is garderobe, or clothes protector. Mix it with dried leaves and flowers of wormwood (*Artemisia absinthum*), rosemary, cotton lavender (*Santolina spp.*), and lavender to make insect-repellent sachets. To scent your clothes, fill a small cotton or muslin bag with any dried moth-repellent herbs, or use aromatic sweet woodruff (*Asperula odorata*), meadowsweet (*Filipendula ulmaria*), or elderflowers (*Sambucus nigra*). Put it in your linen closet.

• In New England, costmary (*Chrysanthemum balsamita*) used to be called the "bible plant," as the flat balsam-scented leaves were used as Bible markers by the Puritans. Costmary, sometimes known as daisy fleabane, has been used since medieval times to protect books from insects. Dry the leaves and insert into treasured books between sheets of tissue paper or use dried sweet woodruff (*Asperula odorata*), which does not mark the pages.

Lavender bags keep bugs from cupboards and drawers and leave a pleasant scent.

TIP

• Make a small mat filled with fleabane (*Gailum verum*) and put it in your pet's bed. Or hang sprays of bog myrtle or sweet gale (*Myrica gale*) above the bed. This is also known as fleawood, once popular for scenting linen and driving out fleas.

• Light scorch marks on rugs can be removed by rubbing with the cut edge of a raw onion.

Make sweet-smelling sachets from aromatic herbs and flowers to hang in your wardrobe.

METAL POLISH

Step 1
Cover 1 oz (25 g) of horsetail with 1 pt (550 ml) of boiling water.

Step 2
Leave it to infuse for two hours, then bring to a boil and simmer for 15 minutes.

Step 3
Pour this over any metal or pewter articles to be cleaned and let them soak for five minutes.

Step 4
Let them drain dry, then buff the surfaces gently with a soft cloth.

WORMWOOD

ALTHOUGH MOST PLANTS WILL HELP AND HEAL, SOME ARE
STILL SEEN TO BRING BAD LUCK. IF YOU'RE SUPERSTITIOUS,
YOU MAY WANT TO AVOID SOME COMMON PLANTS.

Unlucky plants

LILACS AND SNOWDROPS

Beliefs persist that it's unlucky to bring some flowers indoors.
Lilac *(Syringa vulgaris)* grows beside thousands of American and
Canadian houses, allegedly protecting them from evil spirits, but
if brought indoors this foretells death. In Northern Europe some
say it's not allowed in the house because it was once used to
line graves. Nurses never allow it in a sickroom.

LILAC

MYTH BUSTER

• Hawthorn or May blossom *(Crataegus
spp.)* mustn't be taken indoors in England
because of its "sweet smell of death." It has
recently been shown that trimethylamine, one
of the first products formed when animal
tissues start to decay, is present in hawthorn,
so it really does have the odor of death.

• Broad beans were thought to possess the
soul of the dead. It was believed that acci-
dents were more likely to happen
when broad beans were blossoming and, to prevent bad luck for a
year, home-owners were
instructed to scatter a few broad
bean seeds around the
outside of the house.

MAY BLOSSOM

SNOWDROP

OMENS

The snowdrop *(Galanthus
nivalis)* is also often seen as
an omen of death despite its
beauty. Although it symbolizes
purity, it is said to be unlucky
to bring the flower indoors if
someone in the household is
ill. Flowering currant *(Ribes
sanguineum)* is also an ill
omen if picked, and lily-of-the-
valley *(Convallaria majalis)*
must never venture indoors. In
some areas beliefs linger that
"he who plants lily-of-the-
valley will die within the year."

BAD WEATHER

Where societies rely on the weather, many associated plant superstitions exist. Red, white, and evening campions (Silene dioica) and bindweed (Convolvulus spp.) were among many flowers known as thunder plants in Europe and North America, bringing storms if they were picked. The beliefs were in part spread to prevent people from gathering the plants and damaging crops.

Black walnut (Juglans nigra) was said to attract lightning. American shipbuilders avoided it for this reason, and it was considered dangerous even to carry a stray walnut on board. Black walnut hulls contain a substance that helps eliminate parasites, including woodworm, which was probably how this superstition began.

PERILOUS PICKINGS

Cow parsley (Anthriscus sylvestris/Daucus carota) is reputedly unlucky and must not be picked. Country names include "mother die" and "break your mother's heart." This belief probably arose as a warning to children not to pick plants that resembled the poisonous hemlock (Conium maculatum).

Poppies (Papaver rhoeas) were similarly inauspicious and must not be picked. They are credited with causing headaches, earaches, nosebleeds, and even blindness. Moonseed (Menispermum canadense) was called by Native Americans "thunder grapes" or "fruit of the ghosts," to prevent people picking its poisonous berries, which resemble grapes.

COW PARSLEY

Tales abound around cyclamen and its effect on pregnant women.

CHAPTER 8

SCIENCE & PLANT MAGIC

WE ARE FINDING OUT HOW MANY ANCIENT BELIEFS AND PRACTICES ARE STILL USEFUL TO US AND REALIZING THAT MANY OF THE OLD WAYS OF LOOKING AT THE WORLD DID WORK, EVEN IF THE REASONS GIVEN DON'T MAKE MUCH SENSE TO US TODAY. A LOT OF POISONOUS PLANTS HAVE BEEN LINKED TO MAGIC AND SORCERY. NOW WE ARE DISCOVERING THAT THE SORCERERS MAY HAVE KNOWN BEST ALL ALONG, AS DANGEROUS PLANTS ARE PROVIDING IMPORTANT DRUGS FOR CONVENTIONAL MEDICINE.

SIMILARLY, MANY PEOPLE SCOFFED AT APHRODISIACS AS THE PRODUCTS OF FANTASY OR LEGEND. BUT WHEN WE ANALYZE SOME PLANTS, WE FIND THAT IT IS BIOCHEMISTRY RATHER THAN MAGIC THAT RULES THE WAY THEY INFLUENCE OUR BEHAVIOR.

TODAY WE CAN ACCESS SCIENTIFIC INFORMATION ABOUT MANY PLANTS ONCE SEEN AS THE PROVINCE OF SORCERERS AND WITCHES. THERE ARE OFTEN HIGHLY PRACTICAL REASONS TO KEEP THEM OUT OF OUR GARDENS.

Harmful plants

POISONOUS PLANTS

Many plants once deemed to have supernatural powers are poisonous, so myths grew up around them to frighten people away from picking them. Thorn apple or Jimsonweed *(Datura stramonium)* used to be known as a sorcerer's plant. Its use is now restricted by law, because it can cause delirium or death if ingested. Deadly nightshade or belladonna *(Atropa belladonna)* was another much-feared plant, widely used in European witchcraft. Belladonna contains steroidal alkaloids, which inhibit enzymes in the nervous system and can quickly cause death.

HENBANE

Henbane *(Hyocyamus niger)* was described in the 17th century as "a herb of Saturn, and therefore no wonder if it has some sullen conditions with it." Along with many other dangerous plants it was once used to get rid of worms, and considered most potent when gathered by a virgin standing on her right foot and picking the plant with her little finger! It is not recommended as a garden plant – or to be harvested in such a fashion – today, because it is very toxic. Although helmet flower or monkshood *(Aconitum napellus)* was used by monks as a healing plant, it was also a witch's staple. The root is the most poisonous, but touching any parts of the plant can cause contact dermatitis.

MYTH BUSTER

Deadly nightshade, thorn apple, henbane, and monkshood were traditional ingredients in an ointment witches allegedly rubbed over their bodies to prepare for their gatherings. Today these plants are considered too toxic for home practitioners, but are the sources of several important drugs to combat diseases ranging from asthma to Parkinson's disease.

TIP

• Bittersweet or nightshade *(Solanum dulcamara)* is less poisonous than its European relative, belladonna, but don't try to eat the berries. All nightshades accumulate toxic levels of nitrates.

• If you ingest any part of a poisonous plant, call a poison center or emergency services at once. Old-time wisdom decreed that tea made from butterfly weed root *(Asclepias tuberosa)* causes vomiting to purge all but the strongest poison.

DEADLY NIGHTSHADE

POISON IVY

TIP

• To alleviate poison-ivy rash, consider a Native American remedy. Steep plants of shepherd's purse (*Capsella bursapastoris*) in water and wash your skin with the liquid. Or apply crushed plantain leaves as an emergency remedy.

• Watch out for garden rue (*Ruta graveolens*) and spurges (*Euphorbia* spp.). They can also cause an allergic skin rash.

• Sweet cicely (*Osmorhiza longistylis*) could be mistaken for poisonous hemlock or water hemlock (*Cicuta maculata*). The harmless cow parsnip (*Heracleum sphondylium*) looks similar but has larger leaves.

IVY

"Leaflets three, let it be" – never pick poison ivy (*Rhus toxicodendron*). More than half the people who touch it suffer an intense allergic reaction, yet once it was believed that swallowing a leaf would confer immunity. The leaves and stems contain an irritant oil called urushiol, which causes a rash or blisters, and often severe itching. Avoid this ivy.

MYTH BUSTER

• "Wash with brown soap" was a traditional remedy for poison ivy rash. This may remove excess sap and prevent a sufferer from spreading the rash further through contact. But the reaction is actually caused by toxic substances in the poison ivy sap combining with proteins in the skin.

• If you enjoy foraging for wild food, be very careful when harvesting fungi. There are no infallible tricks that will identify all poisonous species; silver spoons or coins will not change color as it was once believed. Always take a reliable identification guide with you when harvesting fungi.

POISONOUS FUNGI

HEMLOCK POISON

Hemlock (*Conium maculatum*) is a legendary poisonous plant that causes respiratory failure. Socrates died from drinking it. Its botanical name comes from the Greek *konos* – a spinning top – because of the dizziness the plant's juices cause. The flowers resemble large heads of cow parsley (*Anthriscus sylvestris*/ *Daucus carota*), but the whole plant has a strong pungent odor.

HEMLOCK

ROSES

DON'T SCOFF AT OLD-FASHIONED LOVE POTIONS – THERE MAY BE SOMETHING TO THEM. IF YOU'RE IN NEED OF A ROMANTIC PICK-ME-UP, SEEK HELP FROM YOUR GARDEN.

Aphrodisiacs

A ROSE FOR LOVE

What could be more romantic than the heady scent and lush appearance of a beautiful dark-red rose (*Rosa* spp.)? Just smelling the perfume is guaranteed to bring pleasure. The red rose is perhaps the most ancient, widespread, and best-known symbol of love through different cultures and ages. Emperors filled their banquet halls and fountains with rose petals; country people had their own rose rituals. Today, florists rely on the symbolism to sell millions of red roses as love tokens.

MYTH BUSTER

It's not just talk. When you smell a rose, it affects your whole biochemistry, setting up a chain reaction releasing enzymes that stimulate neurotransmitters that make you feel good and awaken all your senses. In addition to the qualities of the scent, the vitamins, organic acids, and tannins in roses produce specific effects long recognized by herbalists as aphrodisiac. Rose petals may help clear blockages to the female reproductive system and to the sexual organs. They have been used to enhance women's sexual desire and to treat impotence. Aromatherapists use red rose essence to treat a wide range of sexually related difficulties, to increase confidence in those feeling insecure about their sexuality, and to "open up to love and bring your desires into action."

MANDRAKE ROOT

For centuries the mandrake *(Mandragora officinarum)* was universally credited with aphrodisiac powers, because the large, fleshy divided root was said to look like a naked man. It has been both adored and feared: believed on the one hand to promote fertility and wealth; on the other, sterility and poverty. Roots were sold as love charms, and clairvoyants favored mandrake to enhance their powers.

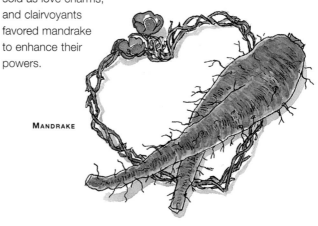

MANDRAKE

• "If women only knew what celery did for men, they would wish for it at every meal." This old saying reflects the long history of celery *(Apium graveolens)* as an aphrodisiac. Celery seeds were among the Romans' favorite aphrodisiac foods. Celery and fennel stimulate digestion, are diuretic, and boost circulation to the sexual organs.

• Peppermint *(Mentha piperita)* was once considered such a strong love potion that ancient Greek soldiers were forbidden to use it in case it distracted them and reduced their courage! For centuries, Arab men drank mint tea for virility. It may be mint's decongestant and astringent qualities that put men in the mood for love.

• Hot peppers are said to increase the "fire" in the body and have long been used to increase sexual energy. The same qualities are ascribed to ginger and other spicy foods. Their heating action opens blood vessels and brings blood nearer to the surface of the skin, which becomes more sensitive to stimulation.

CELERY

MINT TEA

• To add to all its other positive qualities, garlic *(Allium sativum)* is also highly rated as an aphrodisiac and an elixir of youth. Parsley *(Petroselinum crispum)* may have more superstitions attached it than any other plant, so it is little surprise to know it also has an aphrodisiac reputation. It was once much used in love potions for "unwilling" women. Gingko *(Gingko biloba)* is another magic plant. Its seeds are used as a tonic with such varied properties as increasing sexual energy and restoring hearing loss.

• The shape of asparagus *(Asparagus officinalis)* indicates its potential as an aphrodisiac. But beware, because asparagus may do more for men than women. Its main action is diuretic, hence the stimulating effect on the male genitals. But it often makes women yearn for bathroom rather than bedroom!

TIP

Garlic, parsley, and gingko contain substances that help circulation, increase energy, delay aging, and stimulate organs.

PARSLEY

ASPARAGUS

Talking to plants

THERE ARE ALL SORTS OF REASONS WHY PLANTS MIGHT RESPOND TO A GOOD CHAT. WHATEVER YOU BELIEVE, IT CERT-AINLY CAN'T DO ANY HARM, AND YOUR PLANTS MAY REWARD YOU HANDSOMELY.

MYTH BUSTER

• The great American horticulturist Luther Burbank (1849-1926) believed in talking to plants. He bred a spineless cactus, and he believed this had only been possible because he continually talked to his plants, telling them they did not need their defensive thorns because he would look after them.

• The sensitive plant *(Mimosa pudica)* responds to sounds by closing its leaves when confronted with too much noise, but the effect of vibration on plants is usually less obvious. If you recognize, as many scientists do today, that everything is made up of vibrations, or electrical signals, then it makes sense that plants will respond in some way to the human voice.

WHY TALK TO PLANTS?

People have always talked to their plants, both to curse and encourage them. It was once commonly believed every plant had a spirit, which must be praised if the plants were put to use. The old custom of wassailing apple trees and fruit orchards continues today, offering songs and libations to the orchards to ensure a good harvest.

When plants were used as love charms, and in many other old country rituals, they were always acknowledged and celebrated with special rhymes. "Hemp seed I set, hemp seed I sow. The man that is my true love come after me and mow" was a popular 18th century charm. Children still recite "In dock, out nettle, don't let the blood settle" as they rub a nettle sting. In the American Midwest, old-fashioned farmers may still be heard chanting "As big as my butt and as round as my head" as they sow cabbages or turnips, following an age-old tradition requesting a good crop.

THE SENSITIVE PLANT

Grow fantastic flowers by regularly talking to your plants – it's worth a try anyway!

CARBON DIOXIDE

Some people believe talking to your plants helps them grow because you exhale carbon dioxide (CO_2) as you talk to them, providing them with an extra boost of something they need, and they return the favor with some fresh oxygen for you. If you talk regularly to your plants, you are also far more prone to notice changes in them, and know whether they need food or water, or if they are bothered by bugs.

MYTH BUSTER

In some parts of rural Austria, a tradition called *Tonsingen* may still continue. In order to get the best crops, a farmer will throw handfuls of loamy clay into a large barrel of water, stirring first this way, then that, singing a particular series of notes as he stirs. This water is sprinkled over newly sown fields. The singing apparently affects the vibrations in the water and the clay, changing the structure of the water, so it conveys the most possible energy to the young plants to encourage growth.

TOBACCO PLANT

TALKING TO EACH OTHER

Plants talk to their neighbors. Some plants have developed a way of alerting others to potential disease. A virus-infected tobacco plant, for example, can release a chemical signal to bolster its neighbors' resistance. The warning system involves transmitting methyl salicylate, better known as oil of wintergreen, a signaling chemical produced naturally in its leaves. The warning gas travels through the air to a healthy leaf or neighboring plant, where it is converted back into salicylic acid which then encourages the plant to build up antiviral defenses.

Some people believe that plants may even talk to us, declaring they can hear trees screaming as they are felled, or plants crying as they are uprooted. If a person is sensitive to the wavelength at which a plant is vibrating, it may be possible that they could "hear" plants in some way, but the scientific jury is still out on this one.

Bibliography

Bailey, L. H. *The Standard Cyclopedia of Horticulture,* Macmillan, 1956

Baker, Margaret. *Discovering the Folklore of Plants,* Shire Publications, 1996

Boland, Bridget and Maureen. *Old Wives' Lore for Gardeners,* The Bodley Head, 1976

Cherfas, Jeremy, and Fanton, Jude and Michel. *The Seed Savers' Handbook,* Grover Books, 1996

Coats, Alice. *Flowers and their Histories,* McGraw Hill, 1956

Coles, Peggy. *Country Cottage Companion,* David and Charles, 1988

Early American Gardens, for Meate or Medicine. Houghton Mifflin, 1966

Fielder, Mildred. *Plant Medicine and Folklore,* Winchester Press, 1958

Fisher, Robert Moore. *How to Know and Predict the Weather,* New American Library, 1953

Fletcher, H. L.V. *Fletcher's Folly,* Hodder and Stoughton, 1952

Gerard's Herbal, Studio Editions, 1994

Grigson, Geoffrey. *The Englishman's Flora,* Phoenix House, 1958

Grigson, Geoffrey. *Gardenage,* Routledge and Kegan Paul, 1952

Hatfield, Audrey Wynne. *How to Enjoy your Weeds,* Frederick Muller Ltd., 1969

Henderson, Peter. *Gardening for Profit,* The American Botanist Booksellers, 1991

Henderson, Peter. *Henderson's Handbook of Plants,* Henderson and Co., 1881

Inwards, Richard. *Weatherlore,* Pryor Publications, 1999

Lewington, Anna. *Plants for People,* Natural History Museum Publications, 1990

Mabey, Richard. *Flora Britannica,* Chatto and Windus, 1996

Martin, Tovah. *Heirloom Flowers,* Fireside, 1999

McIntyre, Anne. *The Complete Woman's Herbal,* Gaia Books, 1994

McIntyre, Anne. *Simple Home Remedies for Common Ailments,* Gaia Books, 1994

Nancarrow, Loren, and Taylor, Janet Hogan. *Dead Snails Leave no Trails,* Ten Speed Press, 1996

Nancarrow, Loren, and Taylor, Janet Hogan. *Dead Daisies Drive me Crazy,* Ten Speed Press, 2000

Ody, Penelope. *The Herb Society's Complete Medicinal Herbal,* Dorling Kindersley, 1993

Pagram, Beverly. *Natural Housekeeping,* Gaia Books, 1998

Pleasant, Barbara. *The Gardener's Weed Book,* Storey Publishing, 1996

Readman, Jo. *Weeds, How to Control and Love them,* Search Press, 1991

Regel, Pat. *The Houseplant Survival Guide,* Taunton Press, 1997

Rosenstock, Gabriel. *Irish Weather Wisdom,* Appletree Books, 2000

Ryrie, Charlie. *The Healing Energies of Water,* Tuttle, 1998

Schofield, Bernard. *A Miscellany of Garden Wisdom,* HarperCollins, 1991

Seymour, John. *The Self Sufficient Gardener,* Faber and Faber, 1978

Silverman, Maida. *A City Herbal,* Knopf, 1977

Sirasi, Nancy G. *Medieval and Early Renaissance Medicine,* University of Chicago Press, 1990

Stell, Elizabeth P. *Secrets to Great Soil,* Storey Books, 1998

Thompson, C. J. S. *The Hand of Destiny,* Rider and Company, 1932

Thompson's Gardener's Assistant. Gresham Publishing Company, 1901

Tompkins and Bird. *The Secret Life of Plants,* Penguin Books, 1975

Vickery, Roy. *Oxford Dictionary of Plant Lore,* Oxford University Press, 1995

Index

Page numbers in *italics* refer to illustrations

Credits

Quarto would like to thank and acknowledge the following for supplying pictures reproduced in this book. All other photographs and illustrations are the copyright of Quarto Publishing plc.

Key: l left, r right, c center, t top, b bottom

p8 The Art Archive; p9 The Art Archive; p10l J-L Charmet; p10tr J-L Charmet; p10br J-L Charmet; p11t The Art Archive; p12tr J-L Charmet; p13bl J-L Charmet; p13tr J-L Charmet; p14 The Art Archive; p15 The Art Archive; p23t Heather Angel; p24b Heather Angel; p32 Andrew Lawson/GardenImage; p34t Wally Eberhart/GardenImage; p37t Virginia Weiler/GardenImage; p38b John Glover/GardenImage; p43c Virginia Weiler/GardenImage; p44/45t John Glover/GardenImage; p46 Carole Ottesen/GardenImage; p48/49t Nance Trueworthy/GardenImage; p50/51b Harry Smith; p55t Harry Smith; p57t Wally Eberhart/GardenImage; p61t Harry Smith; p66 Mel Wolk/GardenImage; p68l Bob Stefko/GardenImage; p68/69t Ian Adams/GardenImage; p71b Mark Bolton/GardenImage; p72l Mark Bolton/GardenImage; p73t John Glover/GardenImage; p76b Nance Trueworthy/GardenImage; p77b Harry Smith; p78c Mark Bolton/GardenImage; p78/79t Harry Smith; p80c Andrew Lawson/GardenImage; p85r John Glover/GardenImage; p89c Virginia Weiler/GardenImage; p93c Heather Angel; p94c Brian Rogers/Biofotos; p99r Heather Angel; p101l Heather Angel; p106t Dave Bevan; p110/111b Russell Illig/GardenImages; p113t Phillip Roullard/GardenImage; p116 Mark Bolton/GardenImage; p119l Harry Smith; p120 John Glover/GardenImage; p125tl Mel Wolk/GardenImage; p122/123c Harry Smith; p123b Hotshot/GardenImage; p124/125b John Glover/GardenImage; p128 Andrew Lawson/GardenImage; p132/133c Wally Eberhart/GardenImage; p136/137c Mark Bolton/GardenImage; p138r Harry Smith; p139 Harry Smith; p141l Gerald Tang/GardenImage; p143r Virginia Weiler/ GardenImage; p145br Robert Bridges/GardenImage; p145t Harry Smith; p147 John Glover/GardenImage; p154b Harry Smith; p158b John Glover/GardenImage; p160b Harry Smith; p160t John Glover/GardenImage; p164/165b Ian Adams/GardenImage; p165c Gerald Tang/GardenImage; p167b Wally Eberhart/GardenImage; p169b Harry Smith.

Quarto would also like to thank Nursery Trades (Lea Valley) Limited for providing the gardening equipment photographed for this book.

While every effort has been made to credit contributors, Quarto would like to apologize should there have been any omissions or errors.